THE BEAUTIFUL AND THE GOOD.
REASONS FOR SUSTAINABLE FASHION

edited by Marco Ricchetti and Maria Luisa Frisa

XXXXXXXXXXX CENTRO
XXXXXXXXXXX DI
XXXXX   X   FIRENZE
XXXX   XXXX PER LA
XX   XXXXXX MODA
X   XXXX
XXXXXXXXXXX ITALIANA
1954XXXXXXXX

Marsilio

with the collaboration of

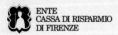
ENTE
CASSA DI RISPARMIO
DI FIRENZE

design
Alessandro Gori.Laboratorium mmxi

picture research
Anita Costanzo

coordination
Serena Becagli.Laboratorium

photographic credits
Bloonie Fotografie
Ilaria D'atri -Lost&Found Studio-
Noë Flum
Christian Geyr
Giovanni Giannoni
Henrik Halvarsson
Daniel Jackson
Jam
Tal Lancman
Alexis Lecomte
Alessandra Leonardi
Nicola Licata
Alasdair Mc Lennan
Raymond Meier
Steven Meisel
Tony Meneguzzo
Jakie Nickerson
Rocco Patella
Terry Richardson
Filippo Ricci
Royah Design Archivio
Mark Schoole
Max Tomasinelli
Luke White

flyleaf picture
reworking of Early Morning Light
in the Forest, ©Sonia Etchison
/ Shutterstock

editiorial assistants
Rosanna Alberti, Paola Gaudioso

translated from the Italian by
David Kerr

acknowledgements
our thanks to

Arturo Andreoni (RadiciGroup)
A.S.A.P.
Banuq
Daniele Beringheli (Maclodio Filati)
B.E.S.T.
Campagna Abiti Puliti
Cangiari
Carmina Campus
C.L.A.S.S.
Fabrizio Conconi (Eurojersey)
Dosa
Ecolabel
Eurojersey
Freitag
From Somewhere
Luisa Cevese Riedizioni
Giannino Malossi
Marvielab
Momaboma
Pietra Pistoletto
Pitti Immagine (for images
of Gentucca Bini)
Royah
Filippo Servalli (RadiciGroup)

first edition July 2012
ISBN 88-317-1260

FSC
Misto
Gruppo di prodotti provenienti da
foreste correttamente gestite e da
altre origini controllate
Cert no. SA-COC-002023
www.fsc.org
© 1996 Forest Stewardship Council

printed on Munken Polar natural paper
made from raw material sourced in
responsibly managed forests or plantations

Contents

7 Foreword
Alberto Pecci

8 Foreword
Angelo Radici

9 The beautiful and the good: A new way (of life) for Italian
fashion?
Alberto Scaccioni

15 ONE. FOUNDATIONS

17 SUSTAINABLE BUSINESS: EDWARD FREEMAN DISCUSSES MANAGING
FOR STAKEHOLDERS
Fabio Guenza

25 ASSESSING SUSTAINABILITY. AN INTERVIEW WITH NICOLE NOTAT
Fabio Guenza

33 A PARADIGM SHIFT IN THE WORLD OF CONSUMPTION AND OF CONSUMERS.
A CONVERSATION ON SUSTAINABILITY WITH FRANCESCO MORACE
Marco Ricchetti

41 IS SUSTAINABILITY WORTH IT?
AN INTERVIEW WITH MARCO RICCHETTI
Franz Tunda

47 TWO. FASHION MATERIALS
DESIGNING FOR SUSTAINABILITY

49 OLD CLOTHES / NEW DESIGN
Elda Danese

57 MATERIALS, PROCESSES, INNOVATION:
SUSTAINABILITY IN THE TEXTILE INDUSTRY
Aurora Magni

75 THREE. MARKETS AND CONSUMERS:
SUSTAINABLE BESTSELLERS

77   **PRACTICES OF SUSTAINABLE FASHION:**
       NIKE AND CARMINA CAMPUS
       Marco Ricchetti and Fabio Guenza

93   **SUSTAINABLE FASHION CONSUMERS HAVE GOT SOLAR PANELS**
       AND DON'T HAVE SEX
       Emanuela Mora, Marie-Cécile Cervellon and Lindsey Carey

109   **FROM THE FASHION FOR GREEN TO GREEN FASHION**
       Lucio Lamberti and Giuliano Noci

119   **FOUR. POLICIES, OBJECTIVES AND TOOLS**
       FOR SUSTAINABLE FASHION

124   **SUSTAINABILITY AND THE FUTURE OF THE ITALIAN FASHION INDUSTRY**
       Marco Ricchetti

133   **LOCAL CULTURES AND SUPPLY CHAINS.**
       BUILDING A NEW ECONOMIC MODEL FOR FASHION
       Giampiero Maracchi

145   **THE LABYRINTH OF LABELS AND CERTIFICATES**
       Lodovico Jucker

159   **TEN KEY STEPS TOWARDS SUSTAINABLE FASHION**
       Fabio Guenza

175   **FIVE. ICONOGRAPHIC ATLAS**
       compiled by Anita Costanzo

177   A............

181   B............

223   C............

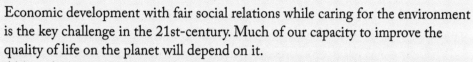

Economic development with fair social relations while caring for the environment is the key challenge in the 21st-century. Much of our capacity to improve the quality of life on the planet will depend on it.

Although the vast majority of people would agree with this claim, our individual behaviour is often in contrast with it. We tend to avoid small and large sacrifices that a coherent approach would call for, believing that "others" should change their behaviour, build infrastructures and introduce measures for the purpose of achieving this objective.

Awareness about sustainable development has spread greatly and consumption has moved in the same direction. The producers' responses, however, have not always been unequivocal. Some capable manufacturers' have provided suitable responses, which have been rewarded by consumers. Others have simply updated their communications, highlighting those aspects of their offerings that are in line with the new awareness without introducing any substantial changes to processes. Others still have actually worked to improve the sustainability of products and processes but have failed to communicate it effectively to consumers.

The sector in which the new consumer culture has produced the most striking results is food. It all began with the logic of healthy foods and the elimination of harmful substances. When this was no longer a distinctive factor, the focus shifted onto production processes and locations and harmony with nature. The results have been achieved thanks also to the development of control systems able to overcome doubts about effective traceability and the authenticity of claims made about properties of products.

By definition, fashion is always well-tuned to consumers' moods and outlooks. The world of fashion has taken on board the significant, widespread desire for eco-friendly products and fair social relationships. But compared to food and other more advanced sectors, the fashion world still lags behind.

For some time now in the world of clothing there have been various initiatives to safeguard producers and consumers. The Pure Wool brand, or Woolmark, for example, is now historic. It was created and promoted by the International Wool Secretariat to guarantee the quality of 100 percent pure wool. One of the best-known and commonly found logos in the world, it effectively set the quality standard.

In more recent times, growing consumer awareness has encouraged the creation of various brands and labels guaranteeing that products meet specific environmental standards in the production process and certifying the authenticity of the raw materials used, the social responsibility of the company, etc.

Unlike what has already happened for food, these often heterogeneous standards and certificates still have major problems in terms of reliability and uniformity. Consumers have difficulty in understanding which labels certify what. The attendant confusion is a major drawback for many businesses in the fashion industry when making investments in sustainability.

On a crowded, bewildering market, there are considerable difficulties involved in communicating the truly sustainable qualities of a product to consumers in a clear and effective way. That is why some companies committed to this kind of strategy have struggled to achieve an effective advantage over those who have not yet committed to sustainability, or simply engage in greenwashing.

Despite the market's considerable, growing awareness, such drawbacks are in danger of barring the way for companies truly interested in going down the path of sustainability and investing in the development of products which, in terms of their content and packaging, meet the needs of many consumers who want "beauty", i.e. to dress in a pleasant attractive way in line with the latest trends while contributing to improving life on the planet and not to its gradual destruction.

The best way to tackle these difficult problems is to begin by unbiasedly framing and illustrating all their various aspects. And in my view that is what this book has boldly and expertly achieved.

Alberto Pecci
President of Il Centro di Firenze per la Moda Italiana

Foreword

Using sustainability as a tool for business, innovation and corporate culture. This is the challenge RadiciGroup is tackling, well aware of the huge environmental, social and economic impact of the activities of an industrial enterprise during its entire life cycle and of the fact that a sustainable approach to doing business can really make a difference. There has been a lot of talk about the green revolution, which is something that affects us all and which must now produce tangible, concrete and clear results. It's time to put words into practice."

Angelo Radici
RadiciGroup Chairman*

*
RadiciGroup has generously supported
the english translation of the book

The beautiful and the good:
A new way (of life) for Italian fashion?

Language also follows fashions. With inevitable flippancy, buzz words become all-pervasive and really do seem to turn up everywhere. One such word is sustainable.

If we read corporate press releases, advertising and interviews, the international fashion world would seem to be deeply committed to battling in favour of the environment through an extraordinary offering of sustainable fashion products: eco-friendly yarns and textiles, green clothes, recycled accessories and ethical and fair production processes. But is this really the case?

When everything becomes sustainable, the term fades to something vague and dull. We thought it was important therefore to try and cast a little light on the subject and understand what we talk about when we talk about sustainability. Moreover, is there an Italian way to sustainability?

We began with some at times awkward questions: is there really a sustainable fashion? And if there is, when is it ethical? When is it fair? When is it really "Made in Italy"? And when is it low cost? In short, is sustainable fashion truly sustainable?

At first glance, the term "sustainable fashion" appears to be an oxymoron or at least a paradox. Fashion is physiologically cannibalistic; it constantly devours itself. It has no time to indulge in distractions not directly involved in the creative process. Yet today fashion communicates an ambition to be eco-friendly. Even the most reputable fashion houses now propose green products and green behaviour at every new season.

And consumers? How do they behave? Is it really true that eco-friendliness has become influential in orienting consumer (and producer) behaviour?

On the subject of consumers, a paradigm that immediately comes to mind is that of the agricultural and food sector, where the terms organic, sustainable, etc., immediately conjure up well-defined brands, regulations and circumscribed areas. One enviable aspect of the food world is the obvious, logical link between issues of health, well-being, the search for healthy life styles and greater attention to the quality of the eating experience and the properties and origin of food. Buying organic food is not a passing fad but part of a philosophy of life focused on respect for your own body and a search for better tasting products. The success of the organic food industry rests on this conceptual pillar and hinged to it are cultural and identity-building operations which are bringing a great narrative power to local areas and the bonds between place, identity and food.

Fashion is still a long way from this paradigm and in the current book we reflect on why this is so. The world of fashion is multidimensional almost in a quantum way: linearity, univocal connections and the cause-and-effect nexus become a luxury, or commonplace.

But how can we recompose this complexity into a narrative? And most importantly, how can we promote it? How can we make it into a strength in the new identity of Italian fashion?

For some time now the Centro di Firenze per la Moda Italiana (CFMI) has been exploring the relationship between fashion and sustainability, intended in both the ethical and environmental sense. This led to the conference in 2009 entitled "Eco-Ethical Fashion. Only a Fashion?". The objective was to highlight the potential of the Italian fashion industry supply chain without overlooking those grey areas which are inevitable in such a fast developing world as that of fashion. The conference conclusions led us to establish a number of key points for those who work in the industry but also for students in the fashion design schools, would-be protagonists of tomorrow's fashion. That's why we wished to produce a book mapping out the conceptual territory and comparing the specific features of the Italian fashion world.

Italy is the only European country with an ancient textile and clothing tradition to have maintained a strong manufacturing system and an integrated supply chain. Almost all other European countries have relocated production of semi-raw material and clothing and accessories overseas and only focus on the distribution of fashion products and services (fairs, fashion shows, etc.). In addition to an industrial system, which is still the reference point for the production of high-end clothing and accessories for the whole world, Italy has also made considerable efforts to preserve an artisan culture with extraordinary manufacturing and at times also artistic skills. The industrial world and the artisan world often converge in Italy: the great designer labels on the global markets in the premium and luxury sectors rely on the qualities, uniqueness, personalisation and tradition that can only be found in craft traditions rooted in local areas. At the same time, more than in the past, artisan values and traditions are now clearly reflected in the big brands' marketing campaigns.

Thanks to this new awareness, today we perceive the relationship with the artisan world not only as concerning exclusiveness and luxury but also as reflecting production enhanced by the values of local community, dignified labour and the conservation of resources – in short the values of sustainability.

We believe that this is enough to justify an independent approach when considering Italy. Moreover, the presence of an integrated supply chain is what may enable Italian fashion to emerge as a genuine paladin of sustainable fashion, since it can control and guarantee eco-friendliness and fair labour in all stages of production. It can be easily demonstrated that the longer the supply chain, the more blurred and difficult controls become as regards underage or illegal labour, cancerogenic dyes, eco-hostile textiles, treatments that are harmful for health, etc. In Italy the supply chain is much shorter, at times almost "zero kilometres" – a very attractive advantage! What if we tried to develop it further?

These considerations bring us to the importance of the consumer: is there a demand for sustainable fashion? How aware is today's fashion consumer?

We know there is no easy, single answer valid for all the various markets: in some countries awareness is very high and purchasing behaviour is already greatly influenced by the sustainable dimension, whereas in other countries there is almost no interest at all.

But what should we in the fashion world aspire to do?

To answer this question, I think of how we purchase food products: when we buy an apple or a sea bass, we ask where the product has come from, how far it has travelled to reach the shop, how it has been preserved, etc. In short we are interested in finding out how authentic and healthy our experience will be when we come to eat the apple or sea bass.

It would be wonderful if we were as equally careful, focused and fair in our assessments when buying an article of clothing or a fashion accessory. The day this happens on a widespread scale, Italy could play a leading role, provided its fashion world is ready to meet the challenge.

Alberto Scaccioni
General Manager of Il Centro di Firenze per la Moda Italiana

global warming

corporate social responsibility

fair trade

ethical labelling

traceability

greenwashing

green marketing

sustainable advertising

slow design/ slow fashion

local production

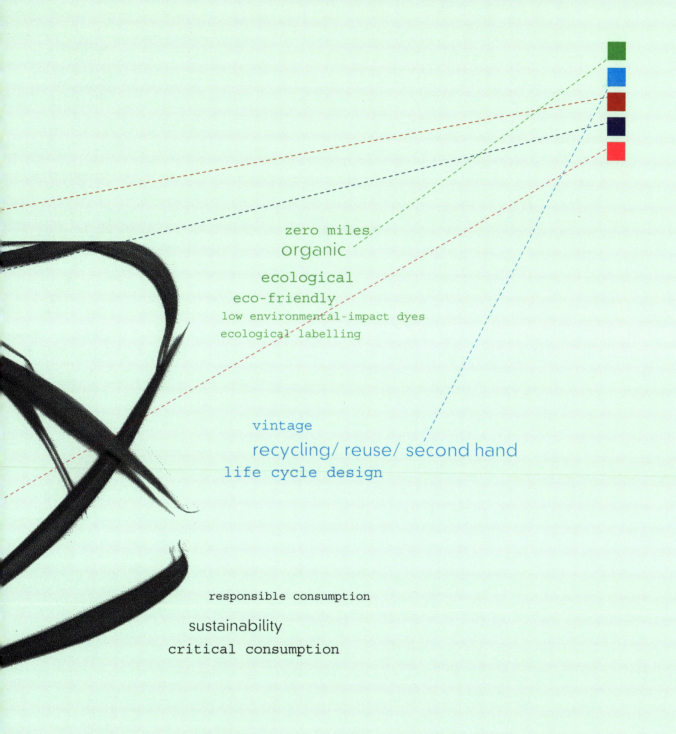

zero miles
organic

ecological
eco-friendly
low environmental-impact dyes
ecological labelling

vintage
recycling/ reuse/ second hand
life cycle design

responsible consumption

sustainability
critical consumption

MAP   13

ONE:
FOUNDATIONS

Profiles of the interviewees

Robert Edward Freeman

Elis and Signe Olsson Professor of Business Administration at the University of Virginia Darden School of Business, Robert Edward Freeman has written over twenty books in the field of management for stakeholders, corporate strategies and business ethics. His latest book *Managing for Stakeholders: Survival, Reputation and Success* is a handbook for managers who wish to develop the capacity to manage relations with stakeholders. His best known work, *Strategic Management: A Stakeholder Approach* has won several awards.

Francesco Morace

A sociologist, writer and journalist, Francesco Morace has worked for over a twenty years in the field of social and market studies. He is president of Future Concept Lab, and head of its research programs: MindStyles, Genius Loci, Street Signals and Happiness. He is a strategies advisor for Italian and international firms and institutions. A lecturer at the Domus Academy and the Politecnico di Milano, he has given talks and held courses and workshops in many countries worldwide. He has also published many books and essays and contributes to magazines in various sectors, such as *Adv*, *Dove*, *Gap Casa*, *Il Bagno*, *Psychologies*, and *7th Floor*; he edits the blog *PreVisioni e Pre-Sentimenti* for *Il Sole 24 Ore*.

Nicole Notat

Nicole Notat is CEO of Vigeo, the leading European agency for the analysis and ratings of companies according to extra-financial indicators. Vigeo analyses corporate performance in terms of sustainable development as well as the social responsibility of asset managers in major investment funds. It conducts social responsibility audits for companies and organisations. Nicole Notat has been secretary general of the Confédération Française Démocratique du Travail (CFDT), chairman of the Conseil de l'Assurance Chomage (UNEDIC), and since 2005 member of the Haute Autorité de Lutte contre les Discriminations (HALDE).

Marco Ricchetti

An economist, since 1989 Marco Ricchetti has been studying the development of export-driven Italian manufacturers and the relations between industrial and creative production in fashion and industrial design. For over ten years he was director of the Federtessile economic studies department. He is an economic consultant and analyst to major Italian fashion organisations, including the Centro di Firenze per la Moda Italiana, Pitti Immagine, Camera Nazionale della Moda Italiana, professional associations in the sector and locally-based industrial and craft associations. He teaches fashion business management at the Politecnico di Milano and the economics of the fashion system at the European Institute of Design in Milan and Venice.

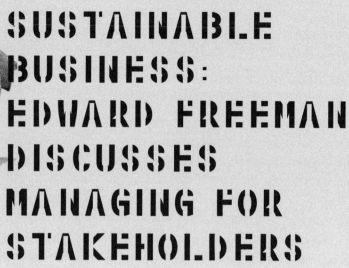

SUSTAINABLE BUSINESS: EDWARD FREEMAN DISCUSSES MANAGING FOR STAKEHOLDERS

Fabio Guenza

The term "stakeholder" is often used in this interview to define a player who can affect and/or be affected by corporate actions. The use of the word stakeholder goes back to a Stanford Research Institute memorandum of 1963. After being used in 1984 to launch Freeman's innovative theory of corporate management, the concept has been widely applied to corporate practice, strategic management theories, corporate governance and corporate social responsibility (CSR). Primary stakeholders are those directly involved in a company's economic transactions: financiers (shareholders, bondholders, creditors, etc), customers, consumers, workers and suppliers. Secondary stakeholders are all those who can affect corporate actions or be affected by them from the environmental, social and ethical points of view: communities, future generations, public administration, activist groups and business associations.

What's the difference between working towards the creation of value for shareholders and the creation of value for stakeholders? Is there a conflict? Is a compromise required?

Some say that the purpose of a business is to make money, to maximize profit in return to shareholders, subject to some constraints such as: how you treat your customers, your employees, what you do in respect of the environment, etc. I think that this is completely wrong. Any business in the world is successful because it can create great products that customers love. If you don't make what customers love, you don't have business – it doesn't matter if we are talking about fashion, automobiles, investment banking or whatever it is. So a business goal is to make products customers love. To do this a business has to have employees who have ideas, who want to make the business grow and develop and who want to make products customers love; you've got to have suppliers who want to work with you, who want to make you a better company. And a business needs finance: financiers, that can be banks, private owners, private equity funds,

17

shareholders. So customers, suppliers, employees and financers are all necessary to run a successful business. Ultimately a business has to have communities, because if there is no support of a community, sooner or later the community will constrain the business and it won't have the same freedom to innovate and create. We've had years and years of history of communities and countries constraining businesses because businesses have not paid much attention to communities. So "managing for stakeholders" is just common sense. If you want to be successful with your business, you have to create value for customers, suppliers, employees, financers and communities. Many people see all these interests as in conflict: "If customers are better off, this means less money to shareholders; if employees are paid a little more, less can be given to customers and less for suppliers; if suppliers are squeezed, more profits can be delivered to shareholders; I don't believe in the community, so I can make more money." Again, thinking about it in terms of tradeoffs is a mistake. What's interesting in the stakeholder idea is the jointness of stakeholders' interests. It's about how to make customers' lives better, and also employees' lives better. And how doing that is a win for shareholders. So seeing stakeholders' interests as joint gets you out of thinking that there are constraints on the real business: you've got a new story about business. The idea of business as a bunch of greedy people out competing with each other has not taken us very far.

So what is the role of profit? Profit itself is one of the most misunderstood ideas around. Many think profits as "bad" because of the pre-eminent idea that profits are the ultimate purpose of the business. It's like saying red blood cells are bad. You must have red blood cells to live or to breathe air, but it doesn't follow that the purpose of life is to make red blood cells. Businesses have to make profits to live, profits are necessary to the business, but it doesn't follow that's profits are the purpose of the business.

Having said that, I'm a fan of businesses making profits. Profits, however, are just the outcome, not the purpose. How do you make profits? Again, it's so simple: you've got great products that customers want. You've got employees who want to be part of the business, you've got suppliers who work to make things better. And you've got good citizens, so the government doesn't need to take your profits. If you do that, then surely profit will be an outcome.

As Jack Welch, former CEO of General Electric, once said: "The idea of maximizing profits is a stupid idea: profits are an outcome, not something that you try to do." And that's what's misunderstood. Even Michael Porter and the famous agency theorist Michael Jensen are now saying "corporate responsibility and managing for stakeholders are important too: if you want to maximize profits, then you have to deal also with stakeholders." Again, I would say that a business is there exactly to create value for stakeholders, that's all that really matters.

The role of competition is another key issue. One way to understand capitalism is that it is about competition: when businesses compete with each other, the fittest and most productive survive, then the greatest good for the greatest number emerges. That is our backward reading of Adam Smith. That is not actually what Adam Smith said, however. He actually wrote two seminal books: one is called *The Wealth of Nations*, with the famous passage of the butcher and the baker on the role of self interest as the engine of social well-being; the other one is *The Theory of Moral Sentiments*. In the latter work Smith says we have to be "men of justice". Essentially, markets which don't have men of justice don't work. If you take a narrow economic view, the greatest good for the greatest number is not an outcome of competition, because of all kinds of externalities.

So I think we misunderstand what really makes capitalism work and we need to revise that.

Think about green business. A lot of people seem to think they have something at stake in saying that companies really should be engaged in green business for the sake of the environment: why not say they are doing it because they are making money? To figure out if it's business or it's ethics is an idea flawed by what I call "the separation fallacy". Most of the time the two drivers are joint. Separating out the "ethics part" is a meaningless exercise for those seeking to identify a purely altruistic model, or a purely selfish model. This is a false dilemma that results from a way of thinking that is outdated.

Many years ago I concluded that people are not just self-interested; they are other-regarding at the same time. Every parent knows this: of course people want to do what is best for themselves, but they also want to do what is best for their children, and their families and their communities, and that extends the base of their concerns much wider. So I think questions about whether a business is driven by self-interest or altruistic sentiment are often irrelevant or misleading; as are questions asking whether green business is driven by opportunity or protection of the environment for the future generations.

To come back to competition, I think that what fuels capitalism is that it is a mechanism whereby we can cooperate together to produce something that no one of us can do alone. Competition is important. In a free society, competition gives people options. But the real engine of capitalism is our desire as human beings to cooperate together to create something. Capitalism is based on our desire to create things that make our lives better. Like profit, competition is a second-order problem. What we got wrong is we did the reverse: we said competition is the central theme of capitalism, not social cooperation. Both are important because you're in a free society and people need options. But actually business activity works because we can figure out how we can make something that no one else can. I think that's cool, that's why I would say that capitalism is the greatest system of social cooperation. It's not socialism, it's not other kinds of things, it's business. Business is about how we cooperate to do things together. That's not easy, that's not always talking happy and feeling good – it can be very hard to do sometimes.

How do corporate organisation and the role of management
change when we adopt the principle of managing for stakeholders?

Let me draw your attention to companies that are *purpose driven*. They
often have had charismatic founders, a founder who believed in a purpose. These
companies are very different: their employees are engaged in the purpose of the
business, they don't need a lot of managers telling them what to do. They know
what to do; they're driven by purpose. These companies don't need that sort of
traditional command and control bureaucracy found in lots of companies.
Purpose in a way tends to replace the command and control bureaucracy.
Purpose (and values) is a much more effective way of managing than hierarchy
and control. That's not to say that all command and control goes away; I'm not
arguing that. What I'm saying is if you have workers who are inspired by purpose,
they can figure out how to work together in teams. You don't need somebody
telling them what to do. They're all going to figure it out; they are smart people
who do things inspired by purpose.

I don't think this is a new feature, a sort of *Business Enterprise Management 2.0*.
This has very deep roots. If you go back and read early 20th-century American
theorists you find many of these ideas there. You certainly find them in Peter
Drucker, you find them in *The Functions of Executives* a 1938 book by Chester
Barnard. These are not new ideas, but if you put them together, it is possible to
run a business so that employees are engaged to ensure that customers are loyal.
Some friends of mine considered these kinds of companies in the book *Firms of
Endearment*. What they found in general in these cases was lower gross margins
– employees earned better, maybe they don't squeeze their suppliers – but they
have much higher net margins. Why? Because some of their other expenses are
so low. They spend very little on marketing and what they do is build a very loyal
set of employees and customers, and so the marketing expenses to try to convince
someone that they need their products are very low.

It's not a question of size. I see small companies with purpose, medium companies
with purpose, or big companies with purpose: they all look pretty similar. It's
easier to change a small company that doesn't have a purpose to one that has a
purpose, whereas changing big companies is hard. Certainly in the relationship
between the founder and the product, generally it's a relationship in which the
founder is completely committed to the product. It's not a question of anything
but passion and love. Passion for the product rather than marketing. In a purpose-
driven company managers love not only what they do, but they believe in making
customers' lives better.

What's the relationship between the concepts of managing
for stakeholders and sustainability?

I'm not much of a fan of separating out corporate social responsibility
and sustainability. Suppose you have a great company: customers love your

products, employees want to work with you because you treat them in a way that respects their dignity, suppliers like to work with you because you make them happier, communities want you in their community because you're a good citizen, and your shareholders love you. I have no idea of what socially responsible means out of all these things. And again, is the company doing a great job for all your stakeholders? In my opinion, sustainability is an outcome of the consideration of the interest of customers, employees, suppliers, financiers and communities. Community is a tricky issue here, because it is a very difficult term to pin down with globalization. Consider the number of communities you might be considered part of. It's hard for managers of companies to figure out what communities to want to serve. Moreover, some communities are virtual, some are global. I'm talking about communities of place, which are the local communities, that's where the employees live and that's where also a few of your customers live. And I'm thinking in particular about the place where the company is located, how the company contributes to building that community and making it better and more attractive, and how doing that also creates value for customers, suppliers, and employees. If you have a particular product that is rooted in a place – Parmesan cheese is a good example in Italy – that product can keep the community strong and wealthy, it creates value.

Sustainability is an outcome that is deeply connected to the time horizon that a company takes in relation to its communities. It makes a great difference if a company has an overall or partial vision of it, if it has a short-term view of these relationships or a long-term view. Ultimately, this is how I think about long term: have a great short term, and keep it up and that way you'll have a great long term.

Fashion is predominantly ephemeral in nature
and at times unjustifiably associated only with luxury and waste.
Does this make the fashion industry less responsible
and less responsive to sustainability?

I think we have to be very careful in saying one business is clearly morally better than another business. Some people say: "This industry is not good, it gives us things we don't need." I'm deeply sceptical of others, especially the state, telling me what I need or I don't need. Ultimately respect for human dignity is about treating people as if they have to make decisions about themselves, even when those decisions are wrong. Now, I can try to educate you so that you shouldn't smoke or you shouldn't eat the wrong food, but ultimately, to treat you with respect for your dignity means: "you've got to make that decision", even when you're going to make a mistake. Likewise, the hardest thing to do as a parent is to let your children make mistakes when you know they're going to make them. I think it's tricky to say: "This is luxury, this is not". It is not relevant to assess if a Ferrari is a luxury good or not, the key question is: "Are stakeholders and communities better off or worse off through its production?" From this point of view, the businesses producing fashion or luxury goods are responsible for the effects of their actions to communities, to customers and to other stakeholders. For how they affect them in exactly the same way as in other industries. If you put responsibility at the centre of the business model, you don't need this distinction between what's a luxury good and what is not.

Having said that, putting responsibility in the centre might mean, for example, that I've got to hunt responsibly. Maybe there are certain species I shouldn't hunt for fashion. What's doing the work here is our sense of being responsible to each other, the awareness of our connections in the world.

What priorities should the fashion industry consider
in order to develop the best possible relations
with its stakeholders and to create value for its communities?

Two closely related priorities in particular come to mind. The first goes back to the companies looked at in the book *Firms of Endearment*. In the costumer and consumer relations companies in the fashion industry rely heavily on brands, with huge marketing costs involved in building and sustaining their brand. *Firms of Endearment* argues that brand value and customer loyalty can be based on the principles of managing for stakeholders. Most of the resources can be better employed in improving products and relations with employees, suppliers, etc. instead of marketing. This would be an interesting stakeholders strategy to think through.

The second priority has to do with the interest conflict between stakeholders. Take for example production relocation. Let's say customers want to pay less for a garment and the producers try to keep their customers happy through reducing costs of production by taking it offshore, thus affecting local workers and communities. In this case we have an interest conflict between costumers, shareholders, employees and local communities. The relocation cuts through the conflict by trading off the various interests in a shortcut that may have very negative effects. As we have seen in the past, a vicious circle is created between customers in search of increasingly low prices and the companies in search of countries with lower costs to satisfy customer interest better and before their rivals. The temptation is to cut corners and make trade-offs, and that can happen. To give in to the temptation, destroying communities and the jointness of stakeholders' interest would ultimately result, I believe, in the slow erosion of Italian fashion over time. In this case management for stakeholders can offer an alternative based on innovation. Businesses have to think differently, to leverage brands that build value on a community of place, on customer well-being, etc. Figuring out how to invent such a business is really important. And it's great that in Italy the industry wants to keep part of the production chain here! Keeping local communities vibrant is a key part of the business model based on management for stakeholders. Innovation can produce unexpected results and mobilise new resources!

Furthermore, I'll never forget what a CEO of a big chemical company said to me: "We're trying to be greener, so we announced a goal of zero pollution." However he was facing engineers claiming: "We'll never do this. This process is too dirty, plant equipment is too old, and we can't meet the environmental standards." The CEO's answer was: "Ok, we've got to close the plant." Engineers came back about three weeks later saying: "It can be done! We've figured it out!" The CEO asked: "Well, how much is it going to cost?" The engineers' answer was: "Well, we're embarrassed to say that if we do things this new way, we're going to save money."

Today in fashion, as in other industries, consumers are demanding sustainability. Do you consider it to be a long-term trend or just... "the latest fashion"?

They are absolutely pushing companies in the right direction! I've never seen a better time to think about creating value for stakeholders than today, partly because smart customers now have a voice; they push companies. The difficulties companies face in order to deliver value to smart consumers is that they really have to innovate. In a command and control hierarchy, that's very hard! That's why you see in these cutting-edge companies, not a command and control hierarchy but people engaged in purpose. Innovation flows from purpose. C. K. Prahalad, one of the greatest strategy theorists, once said: "Creating is a misfit between aspiration and resources." That's a very important concept to grasp for senior executives. We call it "creative stretch". We want aspiration way up, we have resources down, and there is a gap between the two. How do you fill it? When my aspirations overshoot my resources I have to figure out something different! If you have aspiration and I give you all the resources you need to meet it, you don't need much creativity to do that! So the innovation part is what's hard. That's the real challenge.

That's what innovation, and capitalism, are all about! They're about a passion for purpose, and when there's conflict, figuring out how to do it differently. If your starting point is: "Employees can't change, customers can't change, managers can't change..." then in the long run, you're dead! Like the chemical engineers I mentioned, your forced into a creative stretch that leads to innovation.

And the same is true in the fashion industry. The fashion industry is incredibly innovative around questions of design. I don't know if it is very innovative in management organisation or in putting together the interests of stakeholders, but there's a creative artistic part of this, which I believe we have to take into management. When I teach students about leadership – apart from traditional business cases, of course – I talk about literature and music, because leadership is a creative act. It's trying to understand how groups of people engage in a purpose not through controlling but so that they can themselves create communities of people who engage in this purpose. That has more to do with the role of the symphony conductor or the jazz bandleader or the director in a theatre than it has to do with command and control.

A lot of what we have been talking about has to do with the principle of connections. It's one that businesses have forgotten; they often act as markets are the only things that count. Their markets are outside the world, they are distant in some space... The principle of connections is incredibly important, stakeholder interests are connected with businesses, communities are connected, and individuals are connected with others. We need a dialogue between stakeholders and we need to figure it out in a way that's inclusive of others.

Selected bibliography

R.E. Freeman, S.R. Velamuri and B. Moriarty, *Company Stakeholder Responsibility: A New Approach to CSR,* Business Roundtable Institute for Corporate Ethics, 2006, www.corporate-ethics.org

C. Barnard, *The Functions of Executives*, Harvard (Mass.) 2005 [original edn 1938]

A. Smith, *The Theory of Moral Sentiments*, Amherst (NY) 2000 [original edn 1759]

R.S. Sisodia, D. Wolfe and J. Sheth, *Firms of Endearment: How World-Class Companies Profit from Passion and Purpose*, Wharton (Penn.) 2007; see also the *Firms of Endearment* blog: http://firmsofendearment.typepad.com

E.R. Freeman and P.H. Werhane (eds), *Business Ethics*, Malden-Oxford 2005

E.R. Freeman and G. Rusconi, *Teoria degli stakeholder*, Milano 2007

E.R. Freeman, J.S. Harrison and A.C. Wicks, *Managing for Stakeholders: Survival, Reputation, and Success,* New Haven-London 2007

ASSESSING SUSTAINABILITY.
AN INTERVIEW WITH
NICOLE NOTAT

Fabio Guenza

How can we assess a company's commitment and the reliability of its effort in favour of sustainability? Can we adopt objective standards, ratings and rankings as in financial reliability? Or when we talk about sustainability are the results always going to be subjective. Lastly, what happens when we try to assess commitments to sustainability in the fashion world, a sector by definition pervaded with the ephemeral.
We put these questions to the CEO of Vigeo, a leading corporate social responsibility ratings agency.

Madame Notat, you are the founder and chairperson of Vigeo, an agency specialised in assessing corporate social responsibility (CSR). One of Vigeo's distinctive features is the robust objective methodology you have developed to assess companies' efforts to build elements of CSR into their business activities. Can you help us understand what CSR means and how it can be assessed? But firstly, can you tell us how Vigeo came into being?

In my previous job as head of the CFDT (Confédération Française Démocratique du Travail – the French Democratic Labour Confederation), I was able to see how market confidence in some multinationals had been lost because of financial or environmental scandals concerning them. The idea was taking hold that economic aspects were no longer enough to study, assess and run a company, and that the assessment of economic performance could not be separated from considerations of investment risk and sustainability. I realised that there was a latent need for tools to assess those elements of environmental and social responsibility that – although at times intangible – may have an impact on the overall value of a company. This led to the idea of founding a company specialised in assessing corporate social and environmental responsibility.

Adopting a multi-stakeholder approach, I brought into the project stakeholders representing various interests – people from the corporate world, asset managers and associations (unions, NGOs and organisations involved in the social and environmental field). There was a very positive response and the Vigeo shareholders provided the company with a capital of around 17 million euros. This enabled us to attract people with specialist skills in the various fields of corporate social responsibility and to be able to invest in developing a robust methodology.

I would stress that Vigeo has adopted a corporate governance based on ensuring a healthy balance of powers of influence between shareholders. This is a key requisite in guaranteeing the independence that we need in order to pursue our work in a credible way.

Who are Vigeo's services for?

Vigeo's tools are used by pension funds, institutional investors and mutual funds that have decided to consider environmental, social and governance (ESG) aspects in the assessment of investments. This category dubbed "ESG investors" is acquiring increasing importance at European level. For businesses who wish to turn to the capital market, this segment is an extra opportunity to attract financial resources of investors with long-term vision. Vigeo also works with companies to support them in designing corporate strategies and risk management. The results of the assessment requested by companies provide elements to help us understand better the extra financial risks involved. The aim is to implement strategic and operational actions required to guarantee that the company will develop not only profitably but will also be sustainable in the long term.

But isn't there a conflict of interest here? You are helping investors to assess whether to invest or not in a company and at the same time you are offering services to companies.

Services for companies and service for investors are kept very separate. Vigeo is organised in two departments: Vigeo Rating, which deals with services for investors; and Vigeo Enterprise, which provides support to companies. Vigeo Rating's governance and tools ensure the analysts are completely independent and guarantee an objective and transparent rating process.

Our topic is corporate social responsibility, but here we are talking about corporate management, risks and investments. Often there is some confusion over what CSR is really about. What does it mean at Vigeo?

The concept of CSR is open to many, at times discordant interpretations. Today it is still associated with philanthropy and a generic concept of business ethics. These elements are certainly involved in corporate social responsibility but considering them alone, we lose an important dimension.
Corporate social responsibility is a strategic approach to corporate management. Companies' activities generate impacts and expectations on multiple categories of stakeholders. Managing the impact on stakeholders is a means to mitigating risks (to reputation, efficiency, legality, etc.) and a way of creating opportunities and encouraging continuous improvements. With an effective road map to social and environmental responsibility, the company can work towards achieving the objective of sustainability.

This is a very interesting approach but how do you put
such a general principle into practice?

Vigeo's assessment model is the outcome of in-depth analysis of documents, guidelines and declarations drafted by authoritative international organisations, such as the International Labour Organisation (ILO), the UN Global Compact, the United Nations Environment Programme (UNDP), the European Commission, and the Organisation for Economic Cooperation and Development (OECD). Vigeo has long-standing relationships of close collaboration with these international organisations and this has enabled us to identify themes of social responsibility with a universal reach and verifiable objective corporate management principles that explain which actions a company should be encouraged to implement. Vigeo developed a model consisting of assessment criteria and indicators making it possible to compare companies. Comparisons are made between companies operating in the same sector and therefore with similar features and issues. A generic assessment model would not have allowed us to identify which companies effectively develop risk management tools; neither would it have been possible to identify what best practices to adopt.

In the case of the fashion industry, could you give us
a practical example of critical issues?

Identifying themes of social responsibility in a given sector starts from a strategic study of the variables that may generate competitive advantages. In the case of the fashion world there are many such variables. To mention only a few, we have: the control of the supply chain, environmental aspects and all the processes (including sales), quality and compatibility of raw materials and relationships with local communities in developing and developed countries. Take for example the sophisticated specialised skills in producing high-end products. Attracting highly skilled personnel is a problem that both the fashion houses and their suppliers must tackle. It's of vital importance in ensuring an adequate transmission of knowledge from older more experienced staff to the young and also in keeping knowledge constantly updated.

In practice, what does Vigeo assess to establish whether a company is behaving correctly in this sense?

The company must have an training programme honed to the challenges (markets, products, etc.) and their own employees' skills. It must be in a position to be able to make the most of training. Its planning must take into account the time required to attend courses. The company must be able to build up skills by organising internal training courses encouraging the sharing of knowledge and by defining careers that are an incentive for collaborators to improve continuously. These activities should not be seen as a cost or a benefit granted to your own employees but as an investment in human capital.

That's all very well but companies must also reckon with turnover; there is a danger that the investment in human capital could be lost, even to rival companies.

This is undoubtedly a risk. But that's why developing skills must go hand in hand with the capacity to attract and hold onto skilled collaborators. People who work in a company in which the career structure and professional development are clear and transparent will be less interested in changing jobs. We must also take into account the fact that employees have commitments outside work. In a sector with a high concentration of women, developing tools that help reconcile working life and family commitments is crucial. The organisation of work must be planned so as to use flexibility tools, such as part-time working, flexible timetables and working from home. The correct, effective implementation of these solutions enables employees to strike a balance between personal and working requirements, and guarantees greater continuity in the career structure. And this means companies will not lose trained skilled human resources.

When speaking about the development of skills you also mention suppliers. How should a company manage the relationship with its suppliers?

Companies are increasingly dependent on their suppliers because they have very specific skills and are difficult to replace. Often the suppliers are small firms and, although very dynamic, are economically and financially fragile. Suppliers are a resource that must be invested in so as to maintain over time an adequate pool of partners able to meet production requirements in terms of quality and quantity. A large business is in the position to offer suppliers training support, technological updates and, most importantly, financial support guaranteeing their survival even in times of downturns (through appropriate planning of orders and regular payments). Obviously, with a view to a long-term relationship, the supplier receives financial and technical support from the company but in exchange must meet the established social and environmental standards. This applies especially (but not only) to suppliers working in developing countries; in this case a business may be exposed to strong risks threatening its reputation.

But can the risk to reputation justify the costs and complexity of a system monitoring the suppliers?

Accurate monitoring of suppliers also produces benefits in operational terms. Suppliers with better staff management can guarantee higher quality products and greater reliability in deliveries. Moreover, many market research studies show that consumer awareness of social and environmental issues is growing. Consumers are increasingly willing to switch their allegiances to reward socially responsible companies. Our analysts' data highlights the fact that a growing number of companies have committed to a programme of improving social responsibility. At present, not doing so may lead to a loss of competitive advantage and in the medium- to long-term to an erosion of the brand value.

THE VIGEO METHODOLOGY

The Vigeo reference system is divided into six areas of inquiry (see diagram, p. 31). According to the specific nature of the company being analysed and the sector it operates in, the assessment focuses on areas of inquiry and issues considered relevant for the company. Once the issues to be assessed have been defined, standard reference system criteria are selected for each area of inquiry. These criteria are weighted using a algorithm that yields an indication of the social and environmental risk associated with the issue in question. Lastly, each criterion is analysed at three levels:

– A company which must adopt pertinent policies with all-embracing contents in order to show that it has identified the key points of the issue and to give a clear indication of what it means for the company to commit to that issue. The policies must be given suitable visibility inside and outside the company. Lastly, responsibility for the policy must be assigned to people with the power to implement the necessary measures.

– Management systems must be consistent with policies. The processes must be comprehensive and in-built in business activities. Resources allocated to processes (people, tools, skills and investments) must be sufficient to guarantee their correct implementation. Lastly, after start-up, activities must be accompanied by a reporting system to check constantly their effectiveness and to identify areas for improvement. This also makes it possible to establish specific actions to mitigate the areas of risk.

– The last indicator of the quality of corporate commitment is supplied by the results achieved. Stakeholders' opinions are collected through direct interviews or analysed through various media sources (newspapers, specialist reviews and web sites of the main organisations involved in social and environmental issues). Other indications of results are supplied by an analysis of the quantitative data: e.g. an increase in the number of women holding managerial positions indicates a good system of equal opportunities management, or a fall in the employment turnover rate indicates the companies strong capacity to attract and hold onto skilled resource.

A company that manages the social and environmental dimensions correctly will have good policies that translate into efficient management systems; their effectiveness will then be clear from the results achieved.

Some companies may have good policies but they are not reflected in the management processes. Independently of results, these kinds of companies are exposed to risks, because they lack tools for governance and because in case of incidents or controversial episodes their formal commitment exposes them to stronger impacts on reputation. There are also companies that record good results and have good non-formalised management practices in policies and processes. In this case there is less exposure to risk but the lack of a formal system doesn't fully guarantee that all the departments have consistent behaviour and that the current practice will continue unaltered over time.

1.--

Vigeo assessment of social responsibility

Human resources
- Promotion of industrial relations
- Responsible management of restructuring
- Management of careers and promotion of job opportunities
- Improvements to health and safety conditions

Customers and suppliers
- Product security (processes and end use)
- Integration of environmental factors in the supply chain
- Prevention of corruption

Corporate Governance
- Audit and internal control
- Shareholders
- Management remuneration

```
         ↖           ↑           ↗
              ┌─────────────┐
              │   Company   │
              └─────────────┘
         ↙           ↓           ↘
```

Human rights
- Respect for the freedom to associate and the right to collective bargaining
- Non-discrimination

Environment
- Environmental strategy and eco-design
- Prevention and control of pollution (soil, fires, etc.)
- Protection of water resources
- Minimisation of environmental impact of energy consumption
- Management of atmospheric emissions
- Management of transport environmental impacts
- Management of environmental impacts from the use and disposal of products/ services

Local communities
- Promotion of social and economic development

A PARADIGM SHIFT IN THE WORLD OF CONSUMPTION AND OF CONSUMERS. A CONVERSATION ON SUSTAINABILITY WITH FRANCESCO MORACE

Marco Ricchetti

First of all, I would like your view on the context in which the new interest in sustainable consumption has developed.

The essential premise to understanding the phenomenon is that we are experiencing an epoch change. For some decades we talked about an epoch of change, dominated by the ever faster spate of tendencies, a kind of mythology of trends which every year, or almost, implied consumers' passive seduction by new trends. As such these fads had no real substance or foundations. They were the outcome of falling in or out of love with a taste or aesthetics. Basically they were the manifestation of a post-modern sensibility in which everything was relative, and anything could happen. Anything could be changed.

The new paradigm – sustainability is one of its founding value – is based on more stable values. People are no longer satisfied with short-lived frivolous changes. They attribute greater value to the search for a better quality of life. They acknowledge the solidity of the world of the goods that surround us, especially products in the world of fashion, design and food as well as nearly all other everyday objects.

Can you explain a little further what the role of the younger generations has been in this epoch change? How have the younger generations adopted the values of sustainability?

The younger generations were the first to interpret the paradigm shift. They anticipated it and contributed to spreading its values through the new media, social networking, Facebook, etc. They took it on board earlier than the generation of the 30 to 40-year-olds, which had been a driving force in the past. But today the 30-year-olds in particular are weakened by uncertainty about the future and economic difficulties. Today the drivers are mainly the "millennium generation", those born at the turn of the century who are now ten to thirteen. I would include with them their siblings – teenagers and 20-year-olds. It must be said that both sociologists and companies run into difficulty in interpreting young people's behaviour. The sociologists have continued to use outmoded reference models whereby contemporary young people are seen as having no values and are attracted by the empty myths of speed and technology. For twenty years companies, on the other hand, rode the wave of the so-called lightweight generation, addicted to brands and easily influenced. Today the world of young people has changed radically. The epoch change I mentioned can also be applied to interpreting generational developments. Today it's clear, for example, that teenagers no longer feel the need to identify with a brand. They have the tools to make their own choices, possibly in groups, in a gregarious way and these apparently schizophrenic choices are continuously shifting between one taste and another, between one brand and another according to kind of exploratory method. In this context the traditional divisions are no longer valid, including that between classical environmentalism inspired by a "back to basics" niche approach and the majority of consumers, who are keen on playing a leading role through the new values of sustainability.

The younger generations have been involved in elaborating the concept of sustainability much more than the straightforward concept of ecology. Their starting point is no longer an ideal world to be saved, but themselves and the search for happiness, serenity and quality of life. They want to be in the world in a more responsible way. These youngsters have very strong values: friendship, loyalty, transparency and the family. They have renewed their relationships with their grandparents. They have a new relationship with nature and the natural cycles in the biological world. The success of the film *Avatar* is an emblematic example of the meaning of life that goes beyond your own individual ego, of being fashionable or not fashionable. It's about vital energy that goes beyond selfish, personal outlooks and links up to a sense of common destiny. Young people feel this relationship directly with nature rather than making theories or rationalising it.

The fashion world must begin to reflect by starting from this change, destined to grow in the near future. The fashion system has always moved in other more ephemeral worlds where the focus is on creativity and originality. Obviously this not a question of abandoning the nature of fashion – i.e. creative experimentation – but of finding forms enabling us to reconcile the need for a new equilibrium that the younger generations have expressed. The two elements must coexist in a vital way. Following the new paradigms does not mean thinking in a grave rather pompous way or following moralistic-environmentalist models. It means conceiving of fashion that takes into account and interprets a new range of priorities. The current situation can be compared to the hygiene revolution in the late 19th century. A hundred years ago a product that incorporated the new principles of hygiene had a market advantage. Today claiming a product is a market success because it is hygienic doesn't make sense. To reach the markets all products must be hygienic. If they are not, they simply have no market. The same will be happen in the next twenty years with sustainability. Today the sustainability dimension can be seen as an element of differentiation and an advantage for a product. But over the next twenty years, being sustainable will be an indispensable feature that every product must have to reach the market. This evolution is exactly what happens during the paradigmatic shift that marks an epoch change.

A new paradigm takes hold when the majority of consumers and people in general acquire a new awareness about the basic elements of the paradigm, which at that point no product can ignore. Sustainability is and increasingly will be over the next few years a paradigm that companies and politicians will have to act on by responding to the evolution of the collective imagination.

So you think that the focus on sustainability
is not simply the latest fad but will be a permanent factor
in the consumer world?

No question! The real issue is not if it will last or how long, but how it will be expressed as a new founding value. For example, as far as forms of communications are concerned, the value of sustainability will be considered fundamental and taken for granted in any product and so at the same time it will become less important as a distinctive feature in product communications.

How have businesses reacted to the paradigm shift?
Have they already adopted this point of view?
And where do the fashion companies stand,
are they in the forefront or do they lag behind?

The fashion world hasn't been particularly responsive to the new sustainability paradigm when compared to other sectors more directly involved, such as energy, automobiles, industrial design and building. The delay is due to two factors. Firstly, environmental values are peripheral to the clothing competitive map compared to their position in the sectors I just mentioned. Secondly, in the boom of the last thirty years the fashion world created and adopted a very powerful model of relations with the market. It was based on inventing images and dreams rather than referring to real production processes. Calling into question a model that has been successful in the context of the previous paradigm is very difficult. It requires more time and more steps. That's why fashion seems to lag behind in grasping the new features in the latest paradigm. Understandably this is the way it is. As I said, it also depends on the success of the preceding years and not only a structural resistance to the value of sustainability.

We must understand the reasons and act accordingly.

That's why the paradigm shift challenges the fashion world's capacity to tune into the evolutionary spirit of the time. In the past the fashion sector showed it did have this capacity. Today the situation is very different from the previous epoch change, which took place in the 1970s and 80s and which fashion immediately responded to. Indeed ready-to-wear was not only one of the leading players but also a powerful driving force that contributed to freeing us from ideological restraints. Especially in Italy, it offered a new dream. So it's a very difficult for a sector that was once a leader driving the change to accept this kind of condition. The rearguard position also has an interesting aspect, however, and it could turn out to be an advantage. In general, the fashion world has been quick to respond to changes and capable of repositioning itself alongside the leading sectors. The reason for this is that its methods are less affected by institutional factors making other sectors more cumbersome – the automotive sector for example. I believe therefore that in the near future fashion could enjoy an advantage due to this delay. It has not been involved in the stage when the topic of sustainability, for example, was exploited in the environmental field, perhaps in an illusory way, according to old environmentalist modes of thinking. Today fashion companies can adopt a more mature approach by focusing on the production processes and adding its extraordinary creative capacity to the value of sustainability, according to its own genetic code. This might give the notion of sustainability a new aesthetic dignity. Italian fashion could play an important role in the discourse on sustainability. The countries who have clearly been leaders in this role, such as the Northern European countries, Scandinavia, Germany and also Canada, have expressed an aesthetically impoverished and ideologically primitive notion of sustainability, whereby you must give up something to be sustainable. But Italian fashion can inject a sense of enjoyment, thanks to the extra positive value of aesthetic taste and so once more set the pace. This is the great challenge that we must meet.

Do you see advantages and disadvantages for companies in terms of size. Will being small or large make a difference in the drive to make up lost ground?

The usually fairly average size of Italian companies may turn out to be an advantage in the race to win back the leadership. This is precisely for the same reasons that I described as being the principal restraints preventing the fashion world from tuning into the new paradigm. The great retail multinationals and luxury brands, the French for example, are still forced to act according to the rules of the old paradigm. Huge investments in brand building were based on alluding to values and a sensibility that are part of the previous paradigm. They were once the pillars of their success but are now ballast that will be difficult to jettison and will tend to anchor them to the past. The healthy world of Italian companies, on the other hand, can start again from that passion, almost an obsession, that Italian entrepreneurs have always had for the quality of their products. Of course this will only be possible when the new context has been understood. Here I would stress the need for training, to provide companies with certainties. If anything a potential obstacle might be the tendency to imitate the communicative and competitive methods from other business models, such as the great French luxury brands, and not stick to the features of our own industrial system.

I must point out, however, that the kind of company I have in mind is medium rather than small size. These are the "Champions of Made in Italy", as we have called them in studies at the Centro di Firenze per la Moda Italiana. Under a certain threshold, companies – very small firms and micro-firms – don't have the reach to develop a capacity for new ideas in this field.

One example of renewed leadership, based on adopting the new paradigm has been the role played by small and medium Italian companies in the "Slow Food" phenomenon. On a global scale, the movement has been capable of influencing behaviour and informing the collective imagination.

The same thing might happen in the world of fashion.

How is the interest in sustainability
mapped out today. Where, in which places, countries
and continents has it developed most?

Undoubtedly the great North has set the trend with its capacity to translate sustainability into real quality of daily life in only a few years. This has been done, for example, through the re-appropriation of public spaces, often redeveloped thanks to the creativity of Italian or Mediterranean architects who have built projects in countries ranging from Sweden to Canada, or in new areas of the world for them like New Zealand.

It must be said that the values of sustainability have taken hold when they are built into daily life, when they start from people in – I would say – almost a bottom-up process. This is the opposite point of view from that typical of environmentalism, which was strongly connoted in a cultural and ideal direction. One interesting consequence is that the values of sustainability have taken root in parts of the world that are not exactly the most advanced economically. I'm thinking, for example of Brazil. Today it is a country with some of the most interesting social trends, where people realise or feel the importance of these values as a part of their own daily life and as a way of making the most of their own material resources. This link to daily life is thus a very powerful driver encouraging the spread of sustainability on a global scale. It is not limited to Western or economically wealthier countries.

How does this practical daily, non-ideological dimension combine
with the intrinsic need to communicate and inform
about sustainability? Especially considering
that the sustainability content of a product is very often
not immediately perceptible, visible or measurable?

Yes, that's right. One of the founding elements of the new paradigm is credibility. It's an important shift that the fashion world in particular must reckon with.

Firstly, the fashion industry has worked successfully for thirty years almost exclusively on the dimension of visibility – on the image rather than credibility. The important thing was to be present, to have a strong communicational impact, grab the limelight and influence consumers' dreams. The fashion world did this very well by creating its own visual language. It established its own way of looking – see. for example, fashion photography.

Secondly, the aspect of credibility takes us to notions of time and duration. They are in open contrast with the ephemeral aspect of the "fashion system". But this opposition is only apparent. Credibility has been widely worked into the fashion world, for example, in the guise of permanent style. We can argue that Armani's credibility is based on the consistency of his work over time, not simply on the strength of one collection or a seasonal success. Yet again, this may be an advantage for middle-sized Italian companies which, within the fashion world, have been committed to a culture of work pursued constantly over time.

So developing credibility has a twofold meaning. On one hand, it has to do with the temporal dimension. It means maintaining your own character over time. And, on the other hand, there is an interaction with production processes, or rather with the transparency of production processes. Customers want to know where an article of clothing has been made, what materials and processes are involved, who worked on it and in what conditions. Working towards transparency today receives great help from the new media, especially the web and in the monitoring function of social networking in general. A new model of behaviour is thus emerging, whereby you don't give up the aesthetics, feelings and dreams that the fashion world can offer but you demand that all of this is created according to production processes in which the values of sustainability are guaranteed. This brings back us back to a topic I mentioned earlier: passion for the product, which is typical of Italian companies. This passion comes from craftsmanship and survives even when the companies develop industrial structures. The need for transparency, to inform in a step-by-step credible way documenting the features of the production process offers the small and medium-sized Italian companies a great chance to come out of the grey area, where they are often confined, and tell their story of the craft virtues underlying their work. This means a further advantage for Italy companies since today they can still form the whole production chain – albeit with difficulty and uncertainties – from the yarns to the finished product.

This is a chance for Italian companies to restore dignity to the material dimension of care over detail which has always characterised them. Moreover, the old paradigm, with its emphasis on visibility – communication campaigns with top models overshadowing the material features of the product – had confined the material dimension of the product to the background. The small and average-sized companies themselves are often not aware of the value that their passion for the product can generate, if adequately described. At this point the role of a external agent in highlighting this aspect can be useful.

You mention the new media. What do you think their role is?
And what instructions for use would you recommend to companies?

For many companies the first step in the world of the new media was simply to duplicate the usual mono-directional methods of persuasion used in traditional advertising. This was a widespread failure, which highlighted how the new media are not simply another channel with the same rules. They have a different logic. I would add that the impact of this failure was devastating. The persuasive method was immediately unmasked, with often irrecoverable damage to brand credibility.

The great failures have, however, led to the idea that the sophisticated use of the new media can supplement – or in itself be a generator of – customer product appreciation. In this case the idea is that a viral campaign or being in a social network are tools available to companies which per se can create customer communities of product aficionados. This approach tends to force the hand, almost to impose the creation of community. But this is openly at loggerheads with the nature of the new media, which are seen by the people who use them as a tool of individual freedom of expression, i.e. not to be used as an instrument of persuasion or manipulation by a brand. Using the new media means inverting the perspective, as was paradigmatically demonstrated when Barak Obama resorted to it in the last American presidential elections. You don't ask "what a company can do for a social network but what a social network can do for the company!" Communities spring up spontaneously because specific products and brands appeal very strongly to customers. Companies making a successful use of the new media are intelligent enough to take on board and understand the online world that exists independently of corporate communication policies. It exists because people love the product. You can dialogue with this world, you can offer to be a partner, but always by asking "what do *you* want to do for me?". This is a difficult viewpoint to grasp for anyone used to communicating according to the old unidirectional persuasive paradigm.

People in social networks passionate about products are not interested in receiving bargains and gadgets. They're more interested in giving, in being acknowledged as exponents of the brand, of influencing the future development of the product! It must be clear that credibility is created by the product. And its very unlikely that this credibility will be created through the tools offered by the new media. You're kidding yourself if you think that all you need to do is make a Facebook group discuss your company to get customers involved and give your brand credibility.

If not based on product credibility already gained in the field, using the new media only creates straw fires. In short, the new media and the values of sustainability have a common feature: companies can't make an instrumental use of either of them.

IS SUSTAINABILITY WORTH IT? AN INTERVIEW WITH MARCO RICCHETTI

Franz Tunda

What's the relationship between profitability and adopting responsible, sustainable behaviour and practices? How do you reconcile the cost required to adopt them with the quest for profits typical of entrepreneurship in a market economy?

There is a simple answer to this question. If we look at the analogy of the effects on company profits of adopting practices that improve the quality of products, the question is: "How do you reconcile major costs for quality with the quest for profits?"

Ultimately improving the quality of products often, although not always, requires higher production costs. Better and more costly materials can be used to make an article of clothing. Hand-sewing a jacket may require three to four times the work than producing a good but lower-quality jacket made industrially.

But can we say that the profitability of a company will inevitably suffer because of this? If greater quality translates into greater value for the consumers or customers in general, the company's profitability may rise! The same happens with greater costs that may often but not always be incurred by adopting sustainable practices. The idea that there is an inverse relationship, something irreconcilable or even an inevitable conflict between sustainability and profits is mainly due to a vision belonging to an age, that today we can say has almost completely waned. I'm thinking of images like the Greenpeace activists who in the late 1980s launched a big campaign against McDonald's (the McLibel campaign), seen as symbolising the ruthless corporation only interested in profits rather than social values and the environment. Or the activists who in the mid-1990s boarded the Shell-owned Brent Spar oil storage buoy to prevent it from being dismantled and disposed in the Atlantic with very serious repercussions for the marine environment.

This vision of environmentalism that was typical of the last two decades of the previous century is now being replaced by another approach. The new outlook considers the rise of the values of sustainability in close connection to mobilisation within the culture of goods and consumption rather than its rejection.

From this point of view, adopting responsible or environmentally and socially sustainable behaviour is not supported only by a drive towards collective well-being or informed by ideological values (the principle that you do the right thing for the collective well-being, the future of the planet and the establishment of harmonious social relationships). On the contrary, it is seen as a way to economic advantages and profits for companies. In the last three decades, since these notions have become part of the business community vocabulary, a large number of studies have tried to answer the same question you asked me or rather to be more precise: what effect does responsibility and sustainability have on companies' economic and financial results, are they a burden or do they improve profitability?" The results of the studies are not unequivocal. Some have revealed the existence of a negative relationship between corporate social responsibility (CSR) and corporate financial performance. Others have highlighted a positive relationship in the medium term.

How do you account for the difference in results?

The difference in results shouldn't surprise us. Not so much or not only because the differences in opinion between economists on these key questions are rather common, but for the fact that the object being measured is elusive. One of the terms can be defined accurately, even allowing for discussion on suitable indicators, i.e. that concerning the financial performance of companies. But when we come to measure the degree of CSR, we find very different approaches in the available studies.

For example, many studies that found a negative correlation focused mainly on charity activities in educational and health fields, on investments and equipment with low environmental impact, and on opening call centres for customers' complaints. Other studies, which have found a positive correlation, took into account a wider range of factors, including, for example: energy savings or less material waste when sustainability is a priority for the company; the costs of non-sustainability, such as additional taxes or regulations implying bigger costs; the capacity to introduce new products; and a greater overall attention to the relationships with the local communities and customers generating loyalty and improving overall relationships.

In short, what we understand from a survey of the main studies is that the relationship between responsible and sustainable behaviour and profitability is not self-evident and depends more on how the behaviour strategies are implemented rather than the simple fact that they are implemented. And this to a large extent takes us to the way a company relates to all those who share its interests, the stakeholders, of which the most important are the direct customers, suppliers and consumers, workers, shareholders, research centres, media and public administration. A second lesson is that economic advantages do not come from a vague adoption of responsible and sustainable behaviour but are related to the management of specific behaviours and relationships with each stakeholder. The very general definition of sustainable and responsible, is as we said, elusive. The two notions concern an objective towards which we work, for example, by minimising emissions into the atmosphere or encouraging social development, rather than some kind of condition that is achieved once and for all.

The third lesson is the difficulty in benefiting from responsible and sustainable behaviour if it is not systematically followed in all the company's business activities. A significant advantage in relations with consumers built up through actions oriented to sustainability is a heritage that can easily be squandered by an inadequate or off-target communications or marketing policy. The potential of innovation can be thwarted by a rigid corporate structure or strategy that fears the new; potentially high quality work relationships can be inhibited by bad organisation.

Can you give us some examples of the advantages that companies in the fashion world may obtain from careful management for stakeholders?

I know that you will be interviewing Prof Ed Freeman, the leading authority in this field, so I think he will be in a much better position to answer this question in general terms. For my part, I'll try and translate into practical terms seven possible economic benefits of responsible and sustainable behaviour.

1. Responsible and sustainable behaviour influences the relationship with customers and consumers and strengthens the brand image and reputation. This means taking care over customers and material contents (therefore also product quality), innovation and more in general the overall reliability of the brand and of the products themselves. Moreover, since an integral part of sustainability is transparency and dialogue with the consumer, this encourages more interaction and even greater involvement of consumers in the product development processes. The company acquires a more intense, continuous information flow about consumers' wishes and aspirations as well as more brand loyalty and affection. These are crucial elements in the fashion industry, in which the relationship with the consumer is as important as it is unpredictable. In any case transparency and dialogue have not yet been strengths in the fashion world. Indeed, the industry has based its communications more on appealing to consumers' dreams with

powerful images than to their capacity to make choices or by portraying the real substance of production processes.

2. Today sustainability is one of the main vehicles of technological, organisational commercial and cultural innovation. An important part of new products and new production processes have been developed in this field and they can make companies more competitive. A company that pursues sustainability is more likely to come across new ideas that can be developed into innovative products. For example, in the textile industry a large part of research and innovation in the future of new materials, but also in finishing and production processes, has in recent years been informed by the drive to greater sustainability. This is particularly important in the fashion world since every new season brings new products. Fashion companies are particularly responsive to innovation, including innovation informed by the principles of sustainability.

3. The shaping of work relations within a company in a responsible and sustainable way – the definition of rules, procedures and ethical codes and regulations – has positive spin-offs on workers' behaviour, which boosts productivity. Job satisfaction and therefore productivity improves in organisations whose managers are seen as working more fairly and as fulfilling their own commitments and in organisations in which internal rules encourage trust and cooperation. Companies of this kind are preferred by young talents in search of work. A company with a reputation as being a good place to work is more likely to attract the best workers and managers. In the fashion industry this is very important, especially for companies that gamble on tailor-made quality products, and therefore to some extent on handicraft values or the artisanal care even in industrial processes. In this case the value of working relations is at the heart of corporate strategies. This can be seen, for example, in the presence of workers in the company's own advertising campaigns. For companies that make low prices their main competitive lever, on the other hand, and use global production chains with solid bases in countries with low-cost labour, the risks for the brand's reputation in the consumers' eyes are very high when these companies resort to unfair – if not illegal – working practice. Proof of this is the great care that the major world clothing chains now take over such issues by drafting and publicising detailed reports on social and environmental responsibility.

4. In the leather and clothing textile industry, production is in long supply chains made up of independent firms. The production of goods according to sustainable criteria requires a transparent organisation of production process that strengthens bonds and trust between suppliers and producers.

The effects on efficiency in the supply chain and therefore on costs can be positive and fairly significant. Transaction and coordination costs are reduced as is asymmetric information and the dangers of moral hazard.

An important part of the Italian fashion success story has been its system of dedicated industrial "districts". The system of districts is firstly a very powerful way of strengthening relations between companies and generating trust. In this system, geographical proximity and continuous relationships are the main guarantees of fair industrial and commercial relations. Today, when the importance of geographical proximity has partly diminished, the pursuit of greater transparency in relationships, implicit in a sustainable approach, can be a new way of consolidating relationships and generating trust in business to business relations.

5. In fashion and design houses the perception of risk tends to focus spasmodically on the possible failure of new products. This tends to push to the sidelines other important risks generated by non-sustainable behaviour. Brand reputation, often the crucial component in a fashion or designer company's competitiveness is undermined by irresponsible practices, such as employing child labour or using unhealthy toxic chemical substances for leather, for example, thus also generating the risk of huge payments in compensation for damage suffered by customers. Focusing on sustainability is a way of reducing the occurrence of such risks.

6. A strategy driven by sustainability highlights the need to cut some costs, for example, for energy and, thanks to the use of intrinsically less polluting processes, those for purification, which otherwise would not have been carefully analysed. The figures supplied by some big retailers on making savings by analysing energy efficiency are very striking. As regards textile production, some Italian producers of textile machines are significantly now focusing their value proposition on energy savings. In some cases these producers have become much more than machine manufacturers but also all-round consulting companies dealing with all aspects of the green organisation of the production cycle.

7. Lastly, one advantage comes not from the market but from the relations with institutions and society in local communities in general. At a time when regulations to defend the environment adopted by governments in all countries are becoming increasingly tough, companies that pursue sustainability objectives – and therefore that conform to the environmental standards – obtain the right to pursue processes and sell products that those who fail to reach the standards can't. The most advanced practices in the field of environmental sustainability are also those that exercise most influence over decisions concerning future standards, to the advantage of the pioneers. Companies more committed on this front will respond better to public administrations' vision of the industrial future in all countries and therefore may enjoy significant incentives and benefits. The most important examples in the field of textiles and leather concern the use of chemical substances. Initially implemented voluntarily by more forward-looking companies, a ban on toxic substances eventually became compulsory for all companies with the introduction of the European REACH regulations on chemicals and their safe use.

What do you think of the fashion brands' sudden interest
in sustainability? Will it last or will it only be one
of the many passing fads destined to disappear more or less
rapidly?

I will leave the assessment of whether the consumers' interest in sustainability will be long-lasting or ephemeral to the sociologists. I do think, however, that from the point of view of corporate organisation and strategies, the path towards sustainability, by definition, can't be ephemeral. Apart from greenwashing phenomena that may well be ephemeral, pursuing a sustainable policy requires non-recoverable investments and the transformation of the company's organisational structure and its forms of relations with customers and suppliers. So once you begin to go down that path, it's better to go the whole way. In this case too, you only have to make the comparison with the question of quality. Organising a production process according to principles of good quality by cutting down on shortcomings and errors may initially appear costly, but once you have done it, you realise just how much more bad quality cost and so it's not worth turning back.

TWO-
FASHION
MATERIALS
DESIGNING
FOR
SUSTAINABILITY

OLD CLOTHES / NEW DESIGN

Elda Danese*

Latter-day rag merchants

Chronologically fashion has always developed in a non-linear way and has often incorporated the past through stylistic citations and revivals. Today re-appropriation of the past is not only about revisiting old forms. It also involves reusing and recycling by processing existing products, which otherwise would simply have ended up augmenting the already huge volume of waste.

With a radically changed value, the practice of reusing clothes – an anonymous mass of individuals has always been accustomed to wearing second-hand clothes – has entered into the fashion circuit. Once considered a sign of poverty and of belonging to social groups with few opportunities to choose what they can wear, in a different time and place wearing second-hand clothes has become a sign of hostility towards or rejection of the consumer world. This kind of custom has in some ways led to the practice of reusing the inexhaustible reserve of castoffs to create new low-cost styles independently, especially in the aftermath of behaviour arising from youth subcultures. The consequent inclusion of these styles in the fashion industry circuits is due, according to Dick Hebdige, to the need to integrate something that is considered to be different into the shared social fabric.[1]

In the wake of this important way of creating fashion, a new form of historical expertise has emerged: the phenomenon of vintage clothing has led us to distinguish and classify quality even within the enormous heap of used clothes. The positive connotations of vintage mean that the clothes in question are nobler and the fact of ageing has assumed, especially as interpreted by some designers, an aura of romanticism that accompanies the figure of the rag merchant. Recycling thus becomes a kind of metaphor for the redeeming gesture of someone who takes care of what has been abandoned, recognises its beauty and gives it new life. The garment in question bears traces of a story and a past life and that is why, even when produced in series, it is unique and at the same time shared. Martin Margiela, a designer who has interesting thoughts on recycling, expressed the meaning of the operation almost twenty years ago: "When I pick up a piece of clothing that is lying on the ground at the flea market, in the rain, and I transform it, I don't called it destruction. It's great using something that nobody wants any more and making it into a present-day object."[2] One example of this is a sweater made in 1993 from woollen socks picked up in an American army surplus store. The original elements are joined together in a way that creates protuberances in strategic points in the sweater: the elbows, breast, etc. Margiela's attitude, like that of other designers, led him to work in a direction that has shaped a new kind of aesthetics in the field of the fashion design and production never explored until a few decades ago. The possibility of using not only material "as found" but also of working on a deliberate worn-out look for new designer clothes has paved the way to a different kind of glamour – here returned to its ancient etymology as "grammar". Although not the direct expression of an environmentalist awareness, Margiela's designs gave this grammar visibility and the opportunity to spread. Today it is shared by the language of sustainable fashion.

Pietra Pistoletto is another clothes designer working in this area. She has made clothes by recycling various kinds of discarded textiles. Convinced that "the fashion system is now incompatible with the Earth's resources and its ecosystem",[3] Pistoletto designs clothes in an area between art and fashion and focuses on issues associated with the environment. As Antonia Matarrese has stressed,[4] her clothes refer conceptually to her childhood background, to the *Venus of Rags* and the "Zoo costumes" created in the late 1960s by her artist father Michelangelo Pistoletto. In the Pistoletto Foundation at Biella, Pietra is the curator of the Bioethical Sustainable Trend (BEST), the fashion section of the Cittadellarte, an arts and creativity laboratory also dedicated to the development of fashion according to the principles of sustainability. BEST has pursued many initiatives in this direction: from projects dedicated to the promotion of young fashion designers to a platform bringing together various textiles companies involved in eco-friendly production. Katharine Hamnett's strategy of slogan T-shirts, implemented in the 1980s[5] has now been extended to a series of projects moving in the direction of sustainability. We find a similar awareness, albeit with different resources, in those designers who do not recycle used clothes but rather textiles that are discarded after clothes are made. The fascination for scraps and offcuts of precious fabrics has affected many designers. Luisa Cevese collects pieces of fabric left on the looms and includes them in plastic material to make accessories, while Orsola de Castro recovers production process leftovers from high-fashion to make her own collections. In 1987, together with Filippo Ricci, de Castro founded From Somewhere. Based in London, the company produces two collections of clothing using offcuts from fashion producers such as Miles in Vicenza. The company's completely sustainable and ethical supply chain includes a cooperative of disadvantaged people. Each of their models is a unique piece: although the cut is in series, the decoration changes with the way the various materials are assembled. This is a common feature found in many projects dedicated to recycling, since the material strongly affects the appearance and at times the design of the garment. A typical patchwork way of working is a hallmark of their production and at the same time gives rise to an extremely varied output through the combination of the various elements.

Ilaria Venturini Fendi, also uses scraps from other productions, together with more heterogeneous materials, for her collection of handbags. The accessories, jewels and furnishing items of the Carmina Campus association are made one-of-a-kind by craftwork and the variety of the recycled materials. They are conceived to communicate an ethical message and raise awareness about the environment. This is the case of "Message Bags" or the "Cameroon Bags", which are made by women in Dschang, Cameroon, who embroider words and images on recycled materials. A fair trade venture supported by various international organisations, "Cameroon Bags" gives some of the proceeds from sales to construct a study and work centre for African women. The poetics of the citation comes through clearly in the "Save Bags" collection: in this case the black plastic of dustbin liners, doubled up by reinforcing leather, makes a container that is at the same time the frame for a vintage bag. On request, Carmina Campus, will personalise a Save Bag to include a bag supplied by the customer, who in this way shows her own environmental awareness and keeps a loved object in a new form.

Customisation

Carmina Campus Save Bags are an example of a trend to produce personalised objects, with consumers at times also involved in the decisions. The standardisation of industrial products, their reproducibility, are in this case considered as negative values, associated with mass production and waste. With the return to an artisan scale, the one-of-a-kind object acquires greater charm and is made with a special focus on one individual. Manual processing is required in the practice of reusing, to adapt to the specific features of old objects which designers must tackle one at a time. By dialoguing with the past and starting from the pre-existent, they reach a modern form, obtained through various processes: from a fairly simple decontextualising to complete reinterpretation. This has become a widespread practice found both in the essential kind of do-it-yourself recycling and also in the highly sophisticated artisan lines created by some designers. In addition to initiatives like "Made in Mage" (a project conceived to set up critical fashion workshops and ateliers in the former Falck warehouses in Sesto San Giovanni, Milan), some fashion designers have accompanied mass collections with lines based on artisan working and recycling. This is the case with Antonio Marras, who produces one-off garments by reassembling precious vintage material in his "Laboratorio" collection.

One unusual case is Gentucca Bini's idea to reinterpret on the contemporary haute couture scene what was once a common practice among the less well-off classes: i.e. renewing a garment by changing its use. This was a parsimonious measure for survival when repairing and reusing worn out or broken items by sewing was once a commonplace custom. Launched in 2010 at the *Pitti W_ Woman Precollection*, Florence, in the Graanmarkt 13, Antwerp and the Touch!, neoZone and Cloudnine fashion showrooms in Milan, Bini's project involves the designer in personalising clothes from the past. Together with her team that studies and carries out the tailoring, Bini redesigns the old clothes in individual customer's wardrobes and dead stock in fashion houses. This kind of "layering design" superimposes the present on the past, as highlighted by the new label that Bini affixes beside the original brand name. Like many other designers, in this approach she contributes to giving form and widespread visibility to environmental awareness and the desire to reduce waste. Moreover, these kinds of clothes are a badge of belonging to a sustainability project. In this way fashion continues to be a seismograph of social and cultural changes through its capacity to record and react to changes not only in new forms, but also in new approaches to designing.

How do you recognise eco-fashion?

One crucial aspect in the development of green fashion has been the research and policy concerning the elimination of harmful substances from the fibre and textile crop-growing and production stages. The complexity of these processes makes it difficult to find solutions that take into account all the various factors, from protecting the environment to the health of workers and consumers, and from the quality of the material to the cost of the product. Many players in the textiles supply chain are trying to respond positively to the demands of environmentalists. But in the world of fashion, organic quality, sustainable production and ethics are basically not visible in the material. We can easily understand the consternation of Sarah Scaturro – textile conservator at the Cooper-Hewitt National Design Museum, New York – when, on looking with a polarised-light microscope at some threads of her "eco-friendly" sweater made of fibres derived from bamboo, realised that this material was the outcome of production processes and chemical treatment just like that for rayon, one of the most polluting artificial textiles to produce.[6]

Consequently, systems of certification and controls are the principal tools in guaranteeing quality that cannot be distinguished by the senses and in respecting rules established to protect the environment and workers. One crucial part of sustainability in fashion concerns processing fibres, textiles and leather. Public awareness about the relevant data is based more on corporate communications than on recognising the material or on the appearance of a piece of clothing.[7] So how can we tell when fashion is eco-sustainable? In addition to the examples provided above, a significant part of green fashion communications would still seem to lie in the artisan dimension brought into the big cities from those neglected parts of the world that mass consumption has pushed to the sidelines. The end of the great narratives and the breakup of contemporary reality – no longer able to generate utopias and projects of radical social change – have encouraged individual behaviour and specific actions, leaving more room for underground, non-institutional developments: i.e. experiences that are shared in loose associations with open-ended membership. In addition to the consolidated formula of fair trade products, we also have practices combining new design with recycling and the preservation of local traditional techniques from remote, needy areas.

The various aspects of critical fashion tend to bring together production and consumption in a joint project aimed in various ways at reducing waste, the impact on local areas and the exploitation of labour. In some cases the aim is to create situations of cooperation with socially disadvantaged populations and categories. The design of these products – now carefully crafted not to ape folkloric stereotypes – often aims at an identity given by the typical essential nature of traditional clothing and travel wear as well as by highlighting natural materials and dyes. This is the case with a collection made entirely of biodynamic African textiles and natural dyes produced by the Banuq brand (Beautiful African Natural Unique Quality), a company founded in 2008. The African origin of the fibres – exported to be processed to China, India and Switzerland – is emphasised by the recurrent reference to Africa in communications, the frequent presence of coloured models in fashion shows and a series of embellishments and forms which are vaguely ethnic in inspiration, especially as far as female clothing is concerned.

Many projects are created and sustained through private initiatives. There is also a growing number, however, of companies acknowledged and supported by informed institutions in favour of cooperation initiatives in situations of humanitarian or political crises. The "Royah, Clothes Design from Afghanistan" project was set up in 2005 by Milanese designer Gabriella Ghidoni. She is also involved in the actual process of making women's clothing, together with local artisans, who are reviving traditional techniques in the production of precious textiles and embroidery.

Combining forms from Western and Afghan culture, the Royah collections were launched for the first time in Kabul. Since 2006 they have also been presented at events such as Altaroma, Rome, and the Ethical Fashion Shows in Paris and Milan.

Right from the outset the enthusiasm for that culture described in the late 1950s as the "aesthetics of plenty"[8] – it emerged with the growth of Western capitalism in the second post-war period – came in for strong criticism. Moreover, that same culture had paradoxically produced a keen sensibility for recycled material, leftovers and scraps. Central to Dada art, this theme inevitably became even more significant with the parallel growth in industrial mass production. Andy Warhol's remarks on the subject of leftovers are particularly illuminating in this context: "I always like to work on leftovers, doing the leftover things. Things that were discarded, that everybody knew were no good, I always thought had a great potential to be funny. It is like recycling work. I always thought there was a lot of humor in leftovers… I'm saying that what's left over is probably bad, but if you can take it and make it good or at least interesting, then you're not wasting as much as you would otherwise. You're recycling work and you're recycling people, and you're running your business as a by-product of other businesses."[9]

In the interstitial spaces, in the folds of mass production, very different possibilities of life and art forms developed. Radically different points of view gave rise to new experiences based on the rejection of technology and the mass consumption system. Such new approaches aimed to come into contact with a dimension nearer to nature and spirituality.[10] These attitudes of rejection and hostility took on many forms. They spread and were expressed in alternative ways of dressing, eating and forming social relations. Thus, for example, in the 1970s we find the independent American magazine *Rags*. It documented and proposed new ways of clothing, in line with American counterculture attempts to define new forms of expression in what you wear.[11]

The invasion of technology, the rise of an aesthetics of excess – the semantic shift from the aesthetics of plenty in its most mature phase is highly significant – and the global proliferation of consumption models have further encouraged the widespread growth of strongly critical responses. They are fuelled above all by a concern over environmental conditions, the fate of the planet and the inequalities in lifestyles when seen on a global scale. While the radical rejection of consumption was emerging, other currents of analysis tended to explore the possibility of the coexistence of a pervasive consumer culture with a rise in forms involving greater responsibility towards the environment and society.

It was in a certain sense inevitable that fashion would get involved in these problematic issues. In an essay on sustainable fashion, José Teunissen, conservator at the Centraal Museum, Utrecht, claimed: "The quality of products has become more important than the design" and "people prefer wearing classic well-made clothes that are 'authentic' and 'timeless' rather than extravagant products that go out of fashion after just one season."[12]

This statement represents a point of view that has often been reiterated. It sets quality against design as two separate and antithetical entities: the first is the expression of authentic value, the second a trivial skin-deep phenomenon; the first is long term, the second is part of the fast scale of changes in fashion production and increasingly less tuned to social developments. In fact, the qualitative dimension actually comes from design and the lively thinking that accompanies it. This can be demonstrated by the multiple experiments channelled in the direction of sustainability. They seek new solutions through projects that observe and take part in social change.[13] Of course the very idea of authenticity is controversial. Not only in the fashion world but in general, insofar as it is affected by the ever-changing morphology of contemporary reality.

We must also take into account the fact that, although the essence of fashion is change – a phenomena which records and highlights the shifts in contemporary life on the body – the intervals of that change seem to be have become more varied and subjective. To the rhythms of seasons defined by the fashion system, we must add the accelerated timescales of "fast fashion", the deceleration introduced by vintage clothing and individuals' greater independence in deciding when they want to discard items of clothing. In this context we find explorations of a new relationship with clothing, with the value of garments as objects redolent in personal and collective memories. This is not the case with mainstream fashion, which still seems only to offer a mass, depersonalised approach, despite the apparent variety of offerings that should be able to respond to the nuances of contemporary culture. Alternative solutions can be found, however, in vintage clothes, recycling and the emergence of a new widespread artisanal dimension. Indeed the poetics of creative recycling, do-it-yourself, of inventing starting from used or leftover material now permeates the whole contemporary designer fashion scene.

*Faculty of Design and Arts, IUAV, Venice

[1] D. Hebdige, *Subculture. The Meaning of Style*, London 1979, p. 94-96.

[2] "Martin Margiela", in *Journal du textile*, 4 October 1993, p. 57, quoted in *Mutation mode. 1960-2000*, (Paris, Musée Galliera, 1 April-30 July 2000), Paris 2001.

[3] Cf. www.pietrapistoletto.com.

[4] A. Matarrese, in www.pietrapistoletto.com.

[5] C. Breward, "Fashion and Politics", http://showstudio.com/project/politicalfashion/essays/2008-03-03.

[6] S. Scaturro, "Eco-tech Fashion: Rationalizing Technology in Sustainable Fashion", in *Fashion Theory*, 12, 4, p. 470.

[7] On the considerable difficulties encountered by consumers in identifying and purchasing eco-sustainable clothing, see, for example: K.Y. Hiller Connell, "Internal and external barriers to eco-conscious apparel acquisition", in *International Journal of Consumer Studies*, 34, 3, 2010, pp. 279-286.

[8] L. Alloway, "The Long Front of Culture", in *Cambridge Opinion*, 17, 1959, p. 25.

[9] A. Warhol, *From A to B and Back Again: the Philosophy of Andy Warhol*, London, 1975, p.105.

[10] "While the 1950s and 1960s was a period in Europe of, perhaps understandable, acquisition of consumer goods and new technologies after the deprivation of World War Two, the 1970s was a more reflective period, with the embrace of 'flower power' encouraging people to 'drop out' of mainstream consumer society." N.D. Beard, "The Branding of Ethical Fashion and the Consumer: A Luxury Niche or Mass-market Reality?", in *Fashion Theory*, 12, 4, pp. 447-468.

[11] L. Welters, "The Natural Look: American Style in the 1970s?", in *Fashion Theory*, 12, 4, pp. 489-520.

[12] J. Teunissen, "Autisme in de mode", in *Beyond Green*, Arnhem 2008, pp. 18-40.

[13] On this point, see for example: J. Thackara, *In the bubble. Design per un futuro sostenibile*, Turin 2008.

MATERIALS PROCESSES INNOVATION: SUSTAINABILITY IN THE TEXTILE INDUSTRY

Aurora Magni

Textile industry, product life-cycle and sustainability

Although the companies that produce fibres, yarns and textiles are so distant from the places of marketing communications that they are almost always completely unknown, they often contribute in a crucial way to shaping the physical – but also aesthetic and symbolic – features of products that the consumer will buy. These features include those affecting sustainability and especially environmental sustainability. In the absence of a solid material base, the so-called "green" aspect, or more generally the sustainability of a product, tends to be reduced to greenwashing, an ephemeral marketing policy which has little to do with the effective reduction of environmental cost of products. Moreover, spinners, weavers, finishers and workers in other companies employed upstream in the fashion production supply chain now view sustainability as an important factor in making a better offering than their competitors. This is confirmed by the increasingly large presence at textile trade fairs of exhibitors selling eco-friendly yarns and textiles. These products are made with fibres obtained from organic farming, fair trade networks and are treated with natural substances, etc.

Assessing the degree of sustainability of a product requires an evaluation of the whole life cycle, from the cradle to the grave. Analysing the entire production story of a product requires a shift in perspective. A first step in this direction leads us to observe the creation of the product and then to extend the focus to the fashion supply chain and further back to the initial manufacturing processes, such as spinning in the case of textiles or tanning in the leather chain. This is turn leads us to consider the origin of raw materials: farm crops for natural fibres or the production processes for chemical fibres. From this point of view, the textile supply chain must include farm production of vegetable fibres, the raising of fleece animals and silkworms and the process of producing the polymers required for the extrusion stages of man-made fibres. The production conditions of raw materials influence the degree of sustainability of the final product.

Natural fibres

Cotton is by far the most important natural fibre. In 2008 global production was 24,000,000 tonnes, although its overall importance has now been superseded by the family of man-made chemical fibres. In 2009, 42,000,000 tonnes of synthetic fibres were produced. Cotton production requires the use of vast areas of arable land and in some regions of the world it has transformed the local economy into a monoculture, with all the attendant risks. Cotton products, moreover, require large amounts of water. According to recent estimates, the production of 1 kg of cotton clothing requires 9.4 cubic metres of water with peaks of 20 cubic metres if the cotton is grown in countries like India (Gallo 2009). The most striking symbol of the negative impact that the high water consumption in cotton production can have is the almost dried-up Lake Aral in Uzbekistan, whose surface area has been reduced by 60 percent in the last 40 years, while its overall volume of water has fallen by 80 percent. Cotton growing also requires a large use of pesticides and fertilisers with serious consequences both for the environment and the health of people working in the fields. To these we must add CO_2 emissions into the atmosphere generated when transporting the fibres to the spinning, weaving, dying, finishing and production plants, which are often scattered in different areas of the world (Pearce 2009).

The example of the high environmental impact from the production of a natural fibre such as cotton highlights the naivety of the opinion that natural products are automatically eco-friendly or more eco-friendlier than a man-made product.

In recent years many brands in the textile and fashion industry have sent out reassuring messages to consumers about the sustainable nature of their cotton products on the basis of the use of organic cotton. This is a fast-growing trend. Organic cotton has been adopted by some of the major global brands, such as Marks & Spencer, Walmart, H&M and Levi's. Because of its use as a marketing tool and its affinities with the very successful phenomenon of organic food, organic cotton deserves closer examination. Companies often resort to a kind of self-labelling informing customers that their fibres are made with organic cotton, while in other cases they refer to certification issued by third bodies, such as the Istituto per la Certificazione Etica ed Ambientale (ICEA; Institute for Ethical and Environmental Certification), which adopts regulations from international standards such as GOTS (Global Organic Textile Standard). The latter has established regulations for processing organic fibres and includes environmental and social criteria throughout the whole supply chain.

Organic cotton's contribution to the sustainability of textile goods is certainly interesting, but still marginal: certified organic raw material is a minimal percentage of all the cotton in circulation (around 1 percent). Moreover the majority of cotton produced in the world is genetically modified and research into new generation GM cotton is now being conducted (Sala 2005).

Another example of a differentiation strategy based on labelling fibres as sustainable concerns fair trade values, which are informed by a strong social concern and solidarity. In this case the final item of clothing has a production story in which the people determining its sustainability are agricultural communities in low-income countries that supply the raw material generally but not necessarily to non-profit organisations. These organisations then deal with the stages from the production process to marketing the finished product and guarantee its fair trade status. For their part, purchasers are committed not only to paying a fair price but also to providing training and aid to obtain certification – this category includes, for example, the Italian Coop's Solidal (over 430,000 articles sold in 2009). The project has involved local communities in India and Tanzania; the supply chain meets the SA8000 standard of ethical certification and is guaranteed by fair trade certification and the quality brand bioRE* of the Swiss firm Remei Ag.

Other sustainable natural cellulosic vegetable fibres are produced in much smaller quantities than cotton. They include hemp, broom, nettle, bamboo, coconut, maize and soya. Often with ancient traditions, in recent years these easy to cultivate fibres, which can be grown in otherwise arid areas, have seen new developments. Yarns obtained from cellulosic fibres are mainly suitable for furnishing and building and other technical applications although some (bamboo and nettle, for example) have shown that they can be successfully used in clothing, giving the textiles a soft touch and a good degree of comfort (Bacci 2009).

In the case of wool production, the main factors of environmental impact are the consequences of rearing sheep on land and the waste generated by the first stages of processing, especially from washing wool. As far as the first factor is concerned, a positive contribution comes from sheep rearing on barren lands, often not suitable for other kinds of animal rearing or crops. At the same time, however, there are also dangers of desertification of the land caused by intensive rearing. As regards washing wool, the wastewaters from dirty wool washing operations contain polluting substances. To these we can add chemical products used in various stages of processing, from washing (detergents, surface active agents, conditioners, bleaches, etc) to spinning, weaving, dyeing treatments and finishing.

In the case of wool, the markets selling fibres are also very remote from the places of production. Over half the world wool production comes from only three countries: Australia, New Zealand and China. This means that in addition to the environmental impact from processing we must add CO_2 emissions in the atmosphere due to transport from the main manufacturing centres to the shop shelves on the principal consumer markets. Wool, however, is one of the few textile fibres that can be produced at all latitudes, including Europe. In fact an estimated 180,000,000 kilograms of wool are produced in Europe, a far from insignificant amount accounting for just under 20 percent of world wool production. The problem with most of this wool is that it cannot be used for textiles and becomes an environmental cost because it ends up being discarded or in incinerators. Only British wool, just over 30 million kilograms per year, still has a market in the European textile industry, while in Italy wool production amounts to around 15 million kilograms, but according to the estimates of Professor Maracchi, director of the IBIMET-CNR, Florence: "Today 90 percent of wool that is sheared in Italy ends up in the rubbish tips as special waste. The remaining 5 percent is used in the building industry as insulation, or by a few artisans who turn it into felt to make handbags or hats." Paradoxically, moreover, a significant part of Italian wool that does not end up in rubbish dumps is exported to China and India for use in low-quality rugs. The problem with most Italian wool and wool in other continental European countries is that the quality is not high enough for the standards required by the clothing market. The sheep are reared mainly for food purposes (meat and dairy products) and wool is simply a by-product that has to be disposed of in some way, while the Italian textile industry only uses high-quality imported wool. In recent years there has been a new focus on developing home-grown wool both in Italy and in other continental European countries with the twofold objective of exploring new opportunities for use in the textile industry and in promoting better quality wool through improved shearing techniques and wool selection.

Recent initiatives include two particularly significant projects: a Biella CCIAA project in collaboration with the Italian Wool Agency and the Biella Woolcompany; and the "Textiles and Sustainability" project set up by IBIMET-CNR and the Foundation for the Climate and Sustainability, involving the Tuscan Region and the Cassa di Risparmio di Firenze. Both projects have led to the creation of a micro-chain of local or national production that comprises all the stages in the wool production cycle right up to the manufacture of clothing, blankets and other products.

In the field of research, I would mention the studies conducted by ENEA and the University of Camerino to improve the quality of fleece through selection of sheep breeds. Among the more directly business-oriented projects is Lanaitaliana, the brand name of the Lanificio Bottoli, and an initiative still at the design stage called SloWool being pursued by the Lanerossi blanket division in the Marzotto Group. Recent research has also come up with the successful idea of using dirty wool in recovering oil spills at sea (*Il Sole 24 ore*, 31 March 2011).

Biopolymers

Although only a minimal part of oil (around 4 percent) is used in the production of textile yarn (*Assofibre*, CIFRS Italia, 2009), the prospect of its scarcity and especially the low degree of biodegradability of man-made fibres point to the need to make greater use of raw materials from renewable sources (biopolymers). The presence on the derived plastics market of maize starch is a proven example in this sense. In recent years there has been a greater effort on the textiles front in Italy as regards research into renewable materials derived from starch and cellulose or from protein and biodegradable sources, whereby "biodegradability" means the disintegration into organic compounds by means of microorganisms, carbon anhydride, methane, water or biomass.

The increasingly wide use of biopolymers depends mainly on how these materials can be employed as an alternative, at least in part, to synthetic products. Moreover, they may be an economically valid solution to the problem of redeveloping areas otherwise not used by conventional agriculture (also because of the EU "set aside" system to combat surplus food production). At present the main applications of biopolymers are in thermoplastics (i.e. injection-moulded objects for a variety of uses), wall finishes and packaging. Applications are sure to rise significantly, however, and a number of other studies and experiments have been conducted with the aim of introducing textiles with these features onto the fibres market. Moreover, polymers derived from cellulose were first produced specifically for textile applications: they were used in creating continuous yarns, as the industrial history of viscose, acetate or rayon reveals. At the turn of the 20th century many researchers conducted studies on "artificial silk". For simplicity's sake, here we will only consider Count Hillarie de Chardonnet. In 1883 he invented a continuous filament of cellulose origin that can be woven. In the following years he took out forty patents and presented the prototype of a spinning machine at the Paris International Exhibition of 1891. In the 1930s, during Italian autarky, the SNIA produced an artificial fibre called Torviscosa and started up production of Lanital, an invention by the chemist Antonio Ferretti. This revolutionary product extracted from casein was immortalised in 1937 by the Futurist poet Filippo Tommaso Marinetti who dedicated a book to the product (it was also a familiar feature in regime propaganda campaigns): *Il poema del vestito di latte*

("The poem of the milk garment"); the book cover was designed by the young Bruno Munari. In the following decade Lanital was associated with the wholly inadequate poor-quality clothing worn by Italian soldiers on the front. In any case it was soon to be abandoned in favour of new higher performing man-made fibres. In more recent times, however, artificial protein derived from the dairy industry has been tried out again – e.g. the Milkofill® brand products of the Brescia company Filati Maclodio – with some fascinating new results. They range from a high degree of biodegradability to the possibility of making use of waste from other industries, not to mention the interesting, intrinsic features of the material.

There is no lack of protein-based materials from which to extract raw material for new textile substrata (silk, wool and chitosan, for example) and so the world of research and businesses are increasingly interested in polymer extraction. In Italy the Stazione Sperimentale per la Seta ("Experimental Station for Silk") and the CNR Ismac, Biella, for example, are able to produce extremely thin materials with a high degree of porosity through an electrospinning process. These materials can be used in technical textiles (filtering membranes and textiles with modified surface properties) in the biomedical field (scaffolds for tissue growth and vascular prostheses, systems for transporting and releasing drugs) and in the industrial field (reinforcements for composite materials, porous layers for laminate materials, supports for catalysts, etc.). The prospects opened up by biopolymers is one of the most interesting frontiers in the development of fibres and therefore of textile materials. It has, moreover, led to a new model of supply chain in which the textile industry works in close collaboration with other industries, such as farming, intensive animal rearing, the food sector, as well as the chemical industry and the world of research.

From the cradle to the cradle: recycling, the new millennium myth

But what will happen if oil runs short, or if the areas to be used in growing fibres cannot be extended indefinitely and are unable to meet the demand for raw material, especially if in the meantime the world population and related consumption grow in geometric progression?

Part of the solution may come from the heaps of refuse lying in the rubbish dumps around the world waiting to be incinerated or slowly broken down through organic degradation.

Recycling is a term that is increasingly used in conferences and papers dedicated to sustainability and phrases such as "product obtained from recycled material" or "recyclable" now appear on labels for clothing, shoes and accessories. In this paragraph we are not referring to "reusing", but to "recycling" pre-consumer textile materials (i.e. materials from production waste and surplus) or post-consumer materials (recovered at the end of a life cycle), i.e. from a process of transformation aimed at including them in a new production process through preparatory treatment that varies according to the type of fibre.

The term "reuse", on the other hand, refers to the fact of re-employing textiles from used clothes, which are thus given a longer product life cycle, after being regenerated for a new use. In recent years in this field there have been a number of initiatives that have attempted to stimulate ideas and creative solutions to encourage the reuse of clothing. In addition to recovering clothes and giving them to more needy populations, there has been a rise in the number of a second-hand shops and clothes swapping. From this point of view the Internet obviously has an enormous, powerful potential.

Recycling man-made fibres

PET bottles previously used for water and beverages is the best-known example of recycling discarded items to create raw material for a different kind of production from the original. Experience in this field has widely demonstrated how, by selecting and cleaning PET from polluting matter and then by crushing and extruding it, filaments can be obtained for use in making clothing (a classic example is that of pile fabric), padding, nonwovens and composite materials. The recovery of used bottles demonstrates how post-consumer material can be regenerated. This method can now be extended to other contexts to set up specific production chains and technologies (sorting plants, carders and extruders, dyeing plants, etc) able to reduce the still high production costs so that recycled material can be a practical valid alternative to virgin raw materials.

The experience acquired through PET recycling has encouraged some chemical fibre manufacturers to step up their efforts in developing recycling methods for end-of-cycle man-made materials. There are already some encouraging results, such as:

Newlife® – a continuous top-quality polyester yarn produced from a mechanical process for recycling plastic bottles collected in Europe according to a certificated process. The reduced environmental impact and the considerable energy savings have encouraged Filature Miroglio to use post-consumer PET as raw material in the production of a whole range of products. Founded in 1981 as a business exclusively designed to meet the needs of Miroglio Textile, the new company has also become a leader on foreign markets, which now accounts for over 90 percent of its total sales volume. Specialised in the production of continuous thread of polyesters and non-continuous yarn of cotton and rayon, Filature Miroglio now produces 20 million kilograms of yarn, accounting for 20 percent of Miroglio Textile's overall sales.

RadiciGroup – one of the most dynamic Italian multinationals in the chemical and man-made fibres sector. A leading producer of technical polymers with a polyamide and polyester base, today the group has manufacturing facilities and commercial branches in Europe, Asia and North and South America. The company's commitment to sustainability takes the form of policies for energy savings, cutting down the pollution load in wastewater and the production of recycled yarns. Now 100 percent of the nylon polymers made in the group's Italian facilities are produced with hydroelectric energy or through recycling processes.

Sinterama Group – a European leader in the production of threads and yarns of coloured polyester. The company has created Recypes, a polyester yarn obtained from the post-consumer recycling of PET bottles. Its uses include the production of textiles for the seats and door panels in Ford vehicles sold on the US market. The company has manufacturing facilities in Italy, England, Turkey, Brazil and China and every year produces 30,000 tonnes of thread. The innumerable variants of the thread are used in the automotive, furnishing and technical sectors for an overall sales volume of 120 million euros. In 2011, in partnership with the Thai company Indorama Ventures PCL, Sinterama acquired Trevira GmbH, a leading German manufacturer of polyester fibre. Ecozero® – is a thermal and acoustic isolation panel for walls and roofs. CE rated, it is made with polyester fibre obtained from recycling bottles. The producers are Freudenberg Politex, a multinational based in Novedrate (Como), Italy, with manufacturing facilities in Italy, France, the United States and Russia. Together with the Department of Engineering and Physics of the Environment at the University of the Basilicata, the company analyses the environmental impact of its own products and processes using Life Cycle Assessment (LCA) methods. Like Texbond® and Terbond® (bituminous membrane reinforcements), Ecozero® has obtained the Environmental Product Declaration (EPD) label, which certifies the carbon footprint of products and their low environmental impact.

The use of recycled polyesters instead of virgin raw materials has led to a reduction of 50 percent in CO_2-equivalent emissions into the atmosphere. The group's decision to go with clean technology is borne out by its installation of a cogeneration plant in its Novedrate facility, where internal production of electric and heat energy has yielded a further reduction in CO_2 emissions into the atmosphere of around 14,000 tonnes per year. In 2010 Freudenberg Politex was awarded Legambiente's "Eco-friendly Innovation Prize for the South" for its plant at Pisticci (Basilicata).

Recycling natural fibres

Converting rags into regenerated wool is a centuries-old tradition in the textile district of Prato (Tuscany) and arguably the earliest industrial textile business model created round the idea that what is discarded from one technological process can at times be a valuable raw material for another. Recycling rags has enabled the Prato companies (many are involved in the Cardato Regenerated

CO₂ Neutral project, set up in 2009 by the Prato Chamber of Commerce) to acquire technological skills in the selection of materials, treatment of heterogeneous fibres and the use of finishing to improve the look of poor-quality regenerated materials.

The recycling of leftovers from textile production has found receptive markets in various fields for traditional textile applications (building, padding, filters, transport and geotextiles). In fact recycling can generate developments cutting across various industrial sectors. One example is organic building which makes use of textile leftovers in wall structures, heat insulation panelling and flooring. Positive results have been achieved by using discarded hemp, linen and wool. These materials can be heat regulators capable of making walls breathe better and healthier as well as having sound insulation applications.

1. --

Reuse and recycling compared

A) Reuse of clothing and accessories

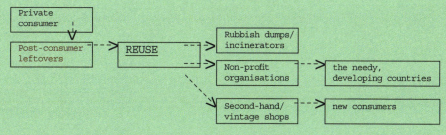

B) Recycling industrial leftovers

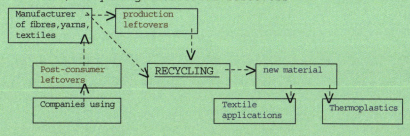

Key: ACTORS | LEFTOVER TYPES | NEW MATERIAL

Production cycle, technological innovation and sustainability

Each stage of processing involves the use of energy, chemical substances and in some cases water, while it generates wastewaters and polluting substances (in the air and in the process waters). Moreover, since many stages in the supply chain are carried out by subcontractors, at times thousands of miles apart, the environmental costs include the often considerable fuel consumption and related pollution from transport as well as packaging required to move the goods.

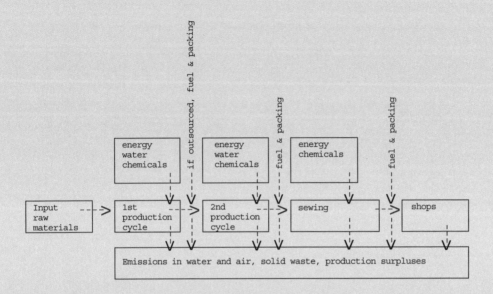

Sustainable textile technology

An important contribution to sustainability comes from the technologies used in processing: machinery and electronic equipment, conveyance systems, purification, filtering and air conditioning plants for the production environments. In recent years manufacturers of textile machines have shifted the focus in research and development from sheer productivity (i.e. greater output and reductions in labour) to new technical solutions such as greater machine versatility and now also water savings and the management of process waste, thus contributing to the overall optimisation of sustainability in the production cycle. Italian textile machinery manufacturers have reiterated their commitment to developing sustainable technology through the Association of Italian Machine Manufacturers for the Textile Industry (ACIMIT – Associazione dei Costruttori Italiani di Macchinario per l'Industria Tessile) with the support of the Ministry for Economic Development and the National Institute for Foreign Trade (ICE – Istituto Nazionale per il Commercio Estero). In 2010 they set up a joint project aimed at developing technological solutions in Italian companies inspired by the values of sustainability. At the Shanghai ITMA Asia + CITME 2010 fair trade, ACIMIT promoted an initiative called "Sustainable Technologies" which brought together and publicised the work and results of around 40 Italian companies involved in the project.

Plasma treatments

Significant innovations in many stages of the production process in favour of greater sustainability have been developed by universities and research centres and are now waiting to be applied in the industrial field. These technologies would contribute significantly to cutting environmental costs, especially in the finishing stages, for example, by drastically reducing the use of process water and the quantity of chemicals required. The most proven innovation is plasma treatment, which can change the properties of textile surfaces at nanometric level. Plasma technologies are based on the principle of activating electrons and free ions which bombard the textile surface. This releases energy to neutral gas molecules and speeds up the chemical processes, which in normal conditions would require large quantities of process water, high temperatures and the use of chemicals. As often happens when innovation is driven by sustainability, the results obtained by plasma technology are twofold: in addition to reducing the environmental impact, the nanometric scale of the process endows the textiles with innovative functional properties that could not have been obtained with the previous technology. They include, for example, greater guarantees about the safety of textiles for users (consumers).

In Italy plasma equipment is in operation not only in research centres like the Stazione Sperimentale per la Seta (Experimental Station for Silk), the CNR-ISMAC, Biella, the Next Technology Tecnotessile Società Nazionale di Ricerca (a national textile technology research society) and the Turin Polytechnic, but also in companies such as Mascioni (specialised in finishing home textiles, the military apparel, sport and protective wear) and Mectex, which produces high-tech textiles used in swimwear and sportswear.

Enzyme treatments

A second interesting area of research focused on reducing the environmental impact of chemical treatments is enzyme processing. This modifies the surface of textiles to obtain, for example, decolouration effects or to modify the feel of a fabric by replacing the usual chemical treatment with less aggressive processes involving enzymes. Enzymes are proteins capable of catalysing chemical reactions in mild conditions of pH, temperature and atmospheric pressure. Safe and easy to control, they act on the specific substrata, speeding up reactions and, most importantly, are biodegradable and reduce costs for chemical substances, energy, water and wastewater treatments.

The natural fibres that have benefited most from the introduction of enzyme processes are cellulosic fibres. Enzyme processes are now commonly applied industrially in treatments for purging and bleaching cotton, for stone washing denims and in various kinds of finishing (removing pilling, softening treatment, etc). The sector of protein fibres (silk and wool) has also benefited from the development of processes based on the use of enzymes, especially in degumming silk and anti-felt treatment for wool.

Lastly, enzyme treatments have contributed to reducing pollutants in process wastewaters and therefore are used in purification plants to speed up the decomposition process.

The list of innovations for sustainability also includes systems for reusing process water, dyeing systems with alternative and waterless processes (for example, in supercritical carbon anhydride), methods for obtaining energy supplies from renewable sources and so on.

Natural dyeing

Techniques of natural dyeing deserve a separate mention. Having fallen into disuse in the 19th century after the development of synthetic colorants, recently a fresh interest has been taken in them by the general public, artisans and even manufacturers.

Firstly, it must be said that using natural substances is a fascinating, intriguing approach to dyeing. Although it is clearly better to use flowers than industrial colorants, they may not be the solution to the problems of sustainability in the dyeing process.

In Italy and the rest of Europe dyeing processes are subject to regulations and restraints imposed by REACH, which has established the rules for the use and sales of dyes, including bans on toxic substances or compounds considered a health risk used in textiles (aromatic ammines, heavy metals, formaldehyde, etc.). The regulations are aimed at protecting the health of workers and end-users of textiles who will inevitably come into contact with them. Leaving aside ideological approaches, several factors are involved in assessing the sustainability of natural dyes:

-origin; hardly any plant crops for natural dyes are grown in Italy, therefore most dyes are imported; stepping up production of vegetable dyes would help to develop underused land and diversify crops (we must bear in mind, however, that any significant increase in these crops could lead, as in the case of biofuel, to a reduction in the areas available for food in poor countries);

−converting plants into dyestuffs requires a special industrial organisation; at present the supply chain is not yet suitably structured. Its environmental impact must be subject to assessment like any other industrial process, whereas the construction of an integrated supply chain natural dyes is still a relatively unexplored but potentially interesting field in Italy.

Further critical points are the instability of natural dyes, which tend to fade during use and washing thus giving garments a worn look (consumers must be aware of this feature when buying a product), and high processing costs, which make them a niche solution employed mainly for high-quality materials and whose strengths lie in personalisation effects and a large degree of biodegradability.

3. Dyeing plants

amaranth	red cabbage	persicaria maculosa
red chard	phytolacca	reseda
calendula	woad	madder
camomile	hypericum	tagetes
hibiscus	nettle	dandelion
carthamus	saffron	

4. Sustainability of the textile and fashion process: areas of action

Raw material	with low ecological impact, or from organic crops from fair trade initiatives from recycling from renewable sources (biopolymers)
Supply chain	energy savings, exploitation of energy from alternative renewable sources recycling of process water and wastewater purification adoption of technologies developed according to eco-principles recycling of leftovers/surplus production elimination of potentially toxic chemicals, search for alternatives
Logistics	rationalisation of transport flows, choice of suppliers also considering proximity; reduced packaging
Promotion	choice of displays; eco-friendly furnishing and lighting systems, less packaging, choice of communications / promotion with lowest eco-impact possible
Use	conditions for washing, stain removal, drying and ironing garments
End of life	reuse garments possibilities of recycling degree of biodegradability; incineration

The company

Eurojersey SpA was founded in the 1970s and specialised in the production of high-quality warp-knit woollen textiles. Since then the company has grown constantly with a great commitment to research and technological innovation for its products and processes. Organised vertically, Eurojersey has an entirely Italian supply chain. Various stages in production are carried out in its Lombardy facility at Caronno Pertusella (Varese): weaving, dyeing, printing, finishing and quality control. This facility also houses the research and development department, style area, sampling and fashion trends departments. Eurojersey currently employs 190 people and has a sales volume of around 60 million euros.

The corporate organisation includes a project manager for sustainability at the head of dedicated work teams. Motivation and participation in the company objectives are encouraged through training and awareness-raising initiatives as well as the overall fostering of a favourable corporate climate.

In 1989 Eurojersey launched Sensitive®, a warp-knit textile made using innovative patented processes. Sensitive® textiles are woven in man-made fibres, lycra and elastomers. They are used in the production of swimming costumes (also for top competitive performances, as in the case of the Speedo Sculpture line), underwear and other sports clothing. In 2007 the company set up SensitivEcoSystem®, an all-round sustainability project which has already yielded practical results, while further positive results are expected in the next few years (www.sensitivecosystem.it).

The example of Eurojersey neatly illustrates two fundamental principles: 1. pursuing sustainability means working on several fronts, from the product to the process, energy consumption and compensatory actions for the environment; 2. communicating sustainability must be clear and not simply allusive; it must go beyond promoting products to businesses and consumers in order to spread a culture of sustainability encouraging coherent behaviour both in consumers and suppliers.

As far as the second point is concerned, in its communications Eurojersey explains these principles in detail and the company takes special care over supplying information and raising awareness both in customers and suppliers. As far as the customers are concerned, the company is committed to the development of sustainability on several fronts.

Sustainability applied to production processes

The first front is that of technology for saving energy and water. Some stages in the Eurojersey production cycle – dyeing, printing and finishing – are typically energy consuming and require large quantities of water. The consumption of energy and process water have been reduced in a number of ways: by adopting an integrated process cycle; by investing in the rationalisation of the logistics to reduce transport movements and related energy costs; and by selecting machines and equipment with low energy consumption. One example of an eco-friendly solution is the Eco Print system, a new technology that interacts with the plain colour of the textile to produce tone-on-tone or contrasting effects. This printing process requires no washing at the end of the cycle and compared to traditional processes brings a saving of 0.19 kW and 50 litres of water for every metre of textile printed, as well as a reduction in process wastewater.

Using renewable energy sources

Eurojersey uses renewable sources for the production of energy. It has installed a photovoltaic solar panel system for the production of energy consumed in office areas. The combination of generating clean energy and energy savings has led to an overall savings of 830,000 kW in the period from 2001 to 2008 (-8 percent).

Recycling

The third front is recycling process water. Savings in water consumption over six years of 88 million litres (-20 percent) has been made possible thanks to an HRS water treatment plant that recycles used water to filter fumes: 7,000 litres of water per hour at a temperature of 85°C are recovered in a storage tank to be used in the production cycle and in the heating plant for the various departments. This process also brings savings on methane of 9.5 percent with a reduction of 1,000 tonnes of atmospheric CO_2 emissions and a calorie savings of around 25,000 cubic metres of unused gas. At the same time the purification plant captures the condensate fumes and in a year collects around 1,500 litres of oil that otherwise would have been dispersed in the atmosphere. Since the entire corporate system must contribute to effective savings of resources, Eurojersey has set up an internal project for separate waste collection and paper saving, which reduced paper used from 2001-2008 by 5 tonnes.

Preservation: protecting the rainforest in Argentina

In addition to direct action to reduce the environmental impact of production, Eurojersey has also supported a number of initiatives conducted by organisations safeguarding the world's environmental heritage. The company has in particular been committed to the conservation of the last rainforests by participating in a project set up in 2010 in collaboration with the World Land Trust, a non-profit making organisation devoted to safeguarding forests. The joint project funds actions to conserve the Yaboti Biosphere Reserve in northeast Argentina, an area of unspoilt Atlantic rainforest with a high degree of biodiversity. The slogan for the initiative is "one metre of fabric for one metre of forest". Eurojersey has thus pledged that for every sqm of Sensitive® textile sold, it will save a metre of forest. Printed on a label on garments made of Sensitive® textile, this message aims to involve consumers as active players in the project. In 2010, the declared objective was to save 3,763 hectares of forest and so link up three parks, the Mocona State Park, the Esmeralda Park and the Parquedo Turbo in Brazil; together they will form a protected area of 60,000 hectares.

Certification

Eurojersey has obtained Environmental Product Declaration (EPD) certification based on Life Cycle Assessment (LCA), i.e. an analysis of a product's environmental impact during its whole lifetime. The standards in question are the UNI EN ISO 14040, 14041, 14042 and 14043 and the Product Declaration drafted according to the specifications of the ISO TC 14025, a voluntary certificate that can be applied to each product. The company is ISO 14001 certified.

THE RADICIGROUP CASE

The company

Radici was created in the 1920s as a commercial company. In 1941 Pietro Radici set up his first manufacturing facility in the province of Bergamo: Tessiture Pietro Radici SpA, specialised in the production of blankets and bed covers. In the 1950s the company began to produce rugs and opened up to man-made fibres by specialising in polymers and synthetic fibres. Following the acquisition of the former Montedison manufacturing facility at Novara, Radici Chimica SpA was founded for the technopolymer market. In the 1990s new businesses were developed, including energy. After an initial investment in cogeneration, Geogreen was created to supply energy and gas to the group and services to outside companies, especially firms operating in the sectors of biomass, thermal and photovoltaic solar energy, wind energy and gas. In 2001 Radici Chimica Deutschland GmbH was founded; it is now one of the most advanced chemical plants in Europe. In 2009 the group had a sales volume of 290 million euros from its chemical area, 132 million from its plastic materials area, 379 million from the synthetic fibres area and 33 million from the textiles area.

The RadiciGroup commitment to sustainability

In 2009 the RadiciGroup for Sustainability programme was set up. Its aim is to "raise awareness in people about sustainability in life styles and working methods, and as a key element in the group's growth." In 2004 the company had already set aside a social budget which in 2009 became the Sustainability Budget, to be used to fund an integrated approach comprising a wide range of actions:
- UNI EN ISO 14001:2004 certification of the Environmental Management System in its manufacturing facilities;
- development and application of technological innovations to reduce emissions;
- energy savings, committing the company to several fronts: reduction in the use of electric energy, the use of methane to produce vapour and the development of energy from renewable sources;
- development of eco-friendly products including: Greenfil®, a high performing yarn created in collaboration with the French company Sofila, proprietor of the brand, which dealt with the texturing process; the RadElast® S RB polymer, a black spandex designed from the outset to have a lower environmental impact than traditional products,

developed with chemical group Arkema; Revive®, a range of polyester products derived from recycling post-consumer PET bottles;

- the application of the Life Cycle Assessment in product development. Thus, for example, a study began to assess the total energy impact (by means of the Gross Energy Requirement indicator) and the contribution to the greenhouse effect of polyamide 66 (by means of the Global Warming Potential, GWP 100) throughout the supply chain to identify the processes with greater environmental impact;

- the systematic adoption of practices useful in reducing environmental impact, from saving paper to the rationalised use of company cars, awareness-raising and training activities for staff and collaborators.

Measurable results

Since 2003 the RadiciGroup has taken part in the Responsible Care® programme. The objective is to gather and publish data on environmental performance in a context of transparency and make continual improvements. The 2009 data reveal that emissions show a downward trend when considered in absolute terms. This trend is partly undoubtedly due to an overall quantitative reduction in products due to the economic downturn. But in most cases, there is also a drop in the relative figure, corroborated by the trend of indicators since 2003. There are still some critical areas and the company is adopting suitable action, especially for emissions from liquid and gas fuel, which in any case are improving, and greenhouse gases. Emissions of heavy metals into the atmosphere have been completely eliminated and their emission into water drastically reduced. As far as water resources are concerned, the use of water has been greatly rationalised. The 2003-2006 trend for the use of mains water shows a substantial reduction in consumption, whereas an even more favourable trend is found in the use of river water, the most important water supply for the companies in the RadiciGroup.

Selected Bibliography

S. Braddock and M. O' Mahony, *Techno Textiles. Revolutionary Fabrics for Fashion and Design*, London 1998.

F. Sala, *Gli Ogm sono davvero pericolosi?*, Rome-Bari 2005.

L. Di Landro, P. Bettini, A. Airoldi and M. R. Pagano, "Tecniche di formatura compositi con fibre vegetali e loro caratterizzazione", XIX Congresso Nazionale AIDAA (Forlì, 17-20 September, 2007).

G.L. Baldo, M. Marino and S. Rossi, *Analisi del ciclo di vita*, Milan 2008.

Progetto Tecnoprimi. Rapporto Finale Nuove tecnologie per il Made in Italy, Paderno Dugnano 2008.

F. Pearce, *Confessions of an Eco-Sinner: Tracking Down the Sources of My Stuff*, Boston (MA) 2008.

L. Bistagnino, *Design Sistemico*, Bra (Cuneo) 2009.

L. Di Landro and W. Lorenzi, "Static and Dynamic Properties of Thermoplastic Matrix/Natural Fiber Composites", in *Journal of Biobased Materials and Bioenergy*, 3, 1-7, 2009.

A. Gallo, "Cotone: Geopolitica di una commodity Agricola", in *Geotema*, 35-36, 2010.

L. Bacci (ed.) *Tessile: sostenibilità e innovazione*, Lamma Test 2009.

"2009. Anno internazionale delle Fibre Naturali", in *Geotema*, 35-36, 2010.

R. M. Dangelico and P. Pontrandolfo, "From Green Product Definitions and Classifications to the Green Option Matrix", in *Journal of Cleaner Production*, 18, 16-17, 2010.

Fibre man-made oltre la crisi: problematiche e opportunità, Assofibre Cirfs Italia, 2010.

Web Resources

www.sustainability-lab.net
www.eurojersey.it
www.sensitivecosystem.it
www.bi.ismac.cnr.it/personale.html
www.tecnotex.it
www.ssiseta.it
www.torinoscienza.it/dossier/funzionalizzazione_di_materiali_tessili_con_plasma_4838
www.worldlandtrust.org
www.filaturemiroglio.com
www.radicigroup.com
www.sinterama.it
www.biellathewoolcompany.it
www.mascioni.it
www.mectex.com
www.freudenbergpolitex.com
www.acimit.it

THREE.
MARKETS AND CONSUMERS: SUSTAINABLE BESTSELLERS

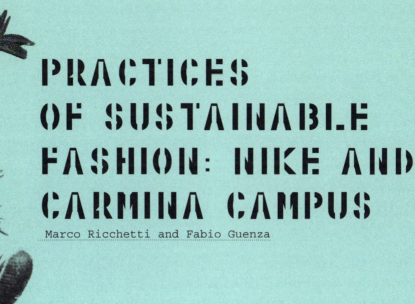

PRACTICES OF SUSTAINABLE FASHION: NIKE AND CARMINA CAMPUS

Marco Ricchetti and Fabio Guenza

A feature that distinguishes the fashion industry from many other manufacturing industries producing consumer goods is the great variety of successful business models. In other words, there is no single philosophy or one optimal business model in terms of size, strategy, product portfolio, positioning and organisational structure. As the saying goes, "one size does not fit all". We thus find considerable differences between market leaders in the world of fashion. And we find the same variety when observing the world of those companies that have boldly set out on the path of sustainability.

Offering a representative survey of the various business models would require a whole book on its own. Here, by means of interviews with representative players, we have tried to tell the story of two cases at opposite ends of the spectrum of possible alternatives.

The first is Nike, the large multinational arguably almost forced into a resolute sustainable strategy after a notorious scandal. Nike has a mass target market and the strength and value of the brand is one of its main competitive levers. In 2010 it ranked 25th in the Interbrand Best Global Brands classification.

The second case is Carmina Campus, a small experimental firm solidly rooted in the fashion business on the high-end luxury market. Founded a few years ago, from the outset the firm has sought to develop a business model focused on sustainability and organised round high-quality products and very advanced stylistic and aesthetic research.

Despite the obvious differences in business models, these two companies share one key point: they are completely opposed to the impoverished ideological vision of sustainable fashion as only being a question of pleasing critical consumers. Both companies believe sustainability is essential in interpreting brand values – i.e. sports performance for Nike, and stylistic and aesthetic experimentation for Carmina Campus.

The interviews are with:

Anna Maria Rugarli. From 1999, she worked for twelve years in the Nike Brussels, Milan and Amsterdam offices, as head of the Department of Public Affairs, Sustainability and Corporate Social Responsibility for the European, Middle Eastern and African region (EMEA).

Ilaria Venturini Fendi and Elisabetta Facco. Designer/founder and head of communications for Carmina Campus, respectively.

The Carmina Campus texts have been supplemented with information derived from the company's documents, summarised by the author of the interviews.

Nike: making a virtue of necessity, and much more

The description of your job at Nike suggests a distinction
between sustainability and corporate social responsibility.
What do these two terms mean for the company?

When I began my career at Nike we used the two terms almost synonymously, but the practical evolution of my job led us to gradually distinguish between sustainability as everything that pertains to the environment and the production and distribution chain, and corporate social responsibility as the activity involving stakeholders, NGOs and institutions in social and environmental projects implemented with local and cross-border communities.

The case of Nike is perhaps the most emblematic
as regards the pressure, tension and contradictions
that can beset the path of sustainability for a fashion company
and its relations with stakeholders. Can you briefly summarise
the development of Nike's sustainability policy
from the beginning to the present day?

As most people know Nike's path to sustainability started from a scandal in 1995-1996. Nike's suppliers had been employing Pakistan children to sow soccer balls. Our initial reaction to the scandal was negative: we couldn't be held responsible for what our suppliers did and relocation was a widespread industrial model. At the time this line of reasoning was shared by most companies but we soon realised that it was short-sighted. We were losing both our reputation and our customers. Our shares were crashing, despite the fact that our accounts were still in excellent shape. We realised two things: for consumers what mattered was not only the final product, the soccer ball, but also the supply chain producing it. In the eyes of the market and public opinion, the scandal could not be justified on the grounds that it was a widespread problem (in fact all sports brands outsourcing in that area in Pakistan were involved). Nike was especially vulnerable for both objective and subjective reasons: because of its world leadership and of its very strong American-style communications. It thus came under fire more than others and the fact that its supply chain problems were exploited was in a way part of the game. Hiding was not our style and shortly afterwards we decided to tackle the critical issues. Nike thus began to dialogue with stakeholders, first in the United States and then in Europe, where they were particularly aggressive. This was the point when I joined the company and had the responsibility of dealing with Europe, but also Africa and the Middle East. The dialogue stage was a great novelty and involved creating discussions with European-wide unions, the major NGOs and some UN agencies. That's why we decided to open an office in Brussels, which was the best place for this kind of networking. Talks then led to an initial operational stage in which we involved the stakeholders in some projects in the supply chain. For the first time what previously had been considered confidential operational information was shared with people outside the company.

The next stage was interiorization and internal reorganisation. It was not enough for the CSR department to dialogue with the stakeholders. Now they had to be involved in the operational divisions – the divisions that had to make the changes. This was very intense work because in practical terms you have to understand the changes required and then modify habits associated with a consolidated model, which the operational managers view as already functioning correctly. These developments led Nike to anticipate the governance of issues of social responsibility in terms of risk management. Thus, for example, there was no longer any need for the company to feature in campaigns on climate change or on CO_2 emissions to begin to get involved in environmental sustainability. Indeed, we realised that this was an opportunity to reaffirm our leadership on the market, strengthen our reputation and so on. If a topic that might concern Nike was on the world public agenda, it was in our interest to put it on our agenda too. So sustainability became a corporate strategy.

It took around fifteen years to reach this "mature phase" in which we continued to raise the stakes for the future, focusing even more on sustainability issues in order to innovate and grow by protecting workers, the environment, consumers and other internal and external stakeholders. We put all of these things into practice in long-term sustainability plans (at present we have a five-year plan begun with a report in 2005–2006, due to expire in 2011). We continually report publicly on the objectives and results of these plans.

As a professional how did you experience this from inside
the company? What skills should a CSR/sustainability
manager have?

When I joined Nike, I was fascinated by these issues but the challenge
really did seem to be a tough one. At the time Nike was still shrouded in
controversy. It took a lot of passion, flexibility and an eclectic approach to
tackle the challenge successfully. But today I'm very pleased with just how far
we've come. At the beginning it was far from easy. My department was seen
almost as an internal NGO or some kind of police outfit. Then we realised that
to collaborate together with everyone, we first had to relate to colleagues in a
different way by looking at the details of their problems and seeking solutions
that were not simply a question of improving the brand reputation but also of
improving their everyday work and economics. In fact we mainly worked out
in the field. Especially at the beginning, we travelled a lot to become familiar
figures and to make ourselves familiar with people scattered round the world
and to understand their issues and so build up relationships of trust. The same
logic applied for both internal and external collaborators, for colleagues and for
NGOs. A turning point came, for example, when the colleagues in the supplies
department agreed to go with us to audit the suppliers, an activity that was
normally carried out by third parties. It was then that I understood something
was changing in our relationship. This was a very important step for them too,
because they could see first-hand the problems they were dealing with. In fact
they were not only dealing with problems of supplies but problems that went
along the way down the line to marketing; we were not, however, mediators
with other departments in the company. We didn't impose a solution because
we knew that our colleagues were capable of seeing how to change their way of
doing things by themselves. Our role was that of facilitator. That's partly why
our structure remained fairly small: just over one hundred people worldwide,
and fifteen in the EMEA.

What kind of dynamics were involved in managing the relationship
with stakeholders? How do they change with geography?
How do you move from a mutually antagonistic approach
to one of collaboration?

What I have outlined so far is the overall development. The story
seen from the inside is much more varied. Every market and community has
different features and priorities, they speak different jargons and even different
languages. A global company must also approach the situation in a personalised
way if it wants to achieve its objectives. To begin with, in some countries there
is more awareness about the environment and in others about workers' rights.
In dialoguing with consumers and the NGOs we must remember that in the
English-speaking world the language is clearer and there is a more widespread

awareness about a company's real functioning and the need to manage risks and seize opportunities. In the Mediterranean area, on the other hand, you have to reckon with a more ideal approach and also with less familiarity with the English language. If you don't make an effort to adapt, you're in danger of not understanding why the people sitting at the table with you are so hostile. You might, for example, only realise afterwards that the information your interlocutors were referring to – Nike only communicates in English – was from years ago but it was the latest thing that had been translated into Spanish. This actually happened!

Moreover, it's difficult to establish a direct relationship with consumers. Very few have the time and tools to form a first-hand opinion by picking their way through the jungle of existing initiatives. The opinion of the average educated consumer is mainly influenced by the media and NGOs. You have to bear in mind that stakeholders' representatives have their own strategies and restraints. The major NGOs are capable of influencing the priorities as perceived by public opinion and therefore the sustainability agenda. But this doesn't always end up reflecting what the real priorities should be. It's important that the NGOs, after the initial stage of denouncing scandals, move on to a stage of collaboration with companies to resolve the real problems, and there must be fairness on both sides. The NGOs are also centres of power. They may have financial problems and as they grow in size and confront reality they may be in danger of losing the kind of ideals that informed their foundation and so adopt more obscure lines of reasoning.

There are many critical aspects of sustainability
but at times the quantity of solutions proposed seems
even greater; there is often a mismatch between supply and demand
for sustainability. How do you choose the right partners
and the right projects?

Today anyone doing my job is subject to a lot of outside pressure and in danger of having to tackle a jungle of very varied initiatives in both the environmental and social fields. At times some are not very valid and others may be not very constructive or simply turn out to be castles in the air. Some are deserving, others are for self-interest. Doing the right thing is crucial so that time and available resources are invested in an effective and efficient way. Some companies may have a kind of database of initiatives, with a rating system based on pre-established criteria. Nike is a hands-on company that also seeks new opportunities. It prefers action to too much thought: "Just do it!".

When people approached me with new initiatives I assessed them case by case. My criteria were simple and practical. They consisted in doing research in the field, going to meet the people and collecting the necessary information to be able to answer a series of questions: "How did the initiative come into being?

What is the history of the NGO in question? Where do the funds allowing it to survive come from? What other companies have they been in touch with, independently of the sector? What do my counterparts think about them?" Anyone doing my job is used to contacting and networking with colleagues in other companies. The fact of being a market leader, proud of your own unique position, does not necessarily mean pursuing certain kinds of initiatives alone. Indeed, if you find yourself alone, you should begin to wonder if you did make the right choice and so you check it out. But this is a downstream problem. Coming back to the upstream decision, the questions I listed are preconditions for establishing a dialogue about what to do. After that you need to compare the proposal with corporate strategies, understand if the initiative will allow you to prevent risks and grasp the opportunities in terms of your own priorities. You must also understand if the project will work as it stands, or if you need to discuss points of compromise between the respective requirements, or even if you wish to make a counterproposal.

We have seen how the projects come into being:
how do they develop after that? What's the relationship
between their evolution and the corporate path
to sustainability?

Even the most successful projects always have a chance element when starting up, especially in an instinctive company like Nike. If the critical issues and priorities are clear, however, it is much more likely that the right idea will arise. Moreover, even the most ingenious idea might be lost if there is not some minimal support structure. Structuring projects means that once you have decided to go with it, you must already imagine its duration, finances and exit strategy. No project will last forever and the time scale varies according to partly predictable but partly unpredictable factors. Some are tactical in nature others strategic and in any case projects are not designed to outlive themselves. The initiatives with NGOs are sustained economically from the initial stage up to a certain point in their development when the budget begins to diminish and they must walk on their own two legs, even by resorting to other sources and forms of funding. Moreover, you have get used to the fact that there are always unpredictable elements. Ideas that initially seem good turn out to be unsuccessful for at times totally unforeseeable reasons. If the human resources are widely involved in the path of sustainability, however, no-brainer ideas can more easily come into being in line with the corporate aim and the projects are understood and supported by the personnel. Nike has developed an integrated process over time in order to involve creative people on the theme of sustainability. When we create a new model of footwear, we have a scoring system that allows you to immediately understand the degree of sustainability of the final product, according to its design features. The system is called the Considered Index and was invented as part of the Nike Considered project by a design team which collaborated both with the traditional design department and the CSR office. The environmental performance, as always, is versed in the language of sport: gold, silver or bronze medals for sustainability accompany the product right up to the end consumer.

Are there some action areas in which it's more difficult to implement projects or on the whole is there not much difference?

The most complex problematic areas are certainly the supply and distribution chains, especially when we are dealing with a sector-wide business model. No matter how important, one company alone can't change the whole industry. At most it can be a leader in efforts to introduce improvements. That's why there are some multilateral initiatives involving cooperation not only with stakeholders but also with rivals and peers, such as, in our case, Adidas, Puma or Gap. Moreover, when we have the same suppliers, the same workers and the same issues, the problems are shared and are in danger of even deteriorating if efforts to solve them, no matter how sincere, are isolated and not coordinated. This was the problem, for example, with codes of conduct. Although similar in reality they were very different in form: different working regulations and different auditors for the same suppliers meant that for a certain period the situation worsened. Only now are we beginning to achieve a certain degree of uniformity. The change requires a collective effort, and then from there on each company can have its own specific approach. Nike's approach is to collaborate closely with the heads of human resources in factories to improve personnel management and therefore at the same time skills, productivity and working conditions.

One important aspect in this kind of development is mutual transparency. In 2005 Nike decided to make public its list of suppliers. But even today some companies still believe this information should be confidential. For Nike too, this move was not without some side-effects, but the company pressed ahead with the decision for two reasons. Firstly, it was an important signal for other companies to encourage mutual collaboration. And, secondly, it was an important message for consumers. By this I mean that although most consumers were not automatically able to understand the significance of this kind of choice, if we do get the message across, many show their appreciation.

What action areas is it easier to implement projects in?

Implementing and communicating sustainable innovation is easier and more direct in the field of the environment. I realised this thanks to projects like Reuse-A-Shoe or the Nike Football Kit. The first is a consolidated programme, although still not very well known in Italy because it could not be introduced here. The project concerns reusing material recovered from sports shoes to make surfaces for playing fields. I believe that, despite all the difficulties of setting up a system with collection points throughout the United States and the complex processing, we were successful because from the beginning to the end we were always tuned into the Nike identity. Every stage and all aspects are to do with sport, even in the sense of giving disadvantaged people the opportunity of playing. Unfortunately, we couldn't introduce this project in Europe, except for the Netherlands and Germany, for logistic, bureaucratic and legal reasons rather than for any question of intrinsic potential. In short, there was not a balance in terms of economics and CO_2 emissions, and the problem was aggravated by the different legislations in the various EU countries.

The second more recent initiative dates back to the 2010 World Cup. Again it is part of the Nike Considered project (it involves the environmental aspects of designing and making products). The project consisted of the production of the Dri-Fit football kits, both those on sale and those worn by soccer players in various countries. This breathing fabric is made of plastic from recycled PET bottles. Nike is an innovative company and sustainable innovation is a good business opportunity. In this case it allowed us to bring together technology, performance and sustainability.

How do you communicate the results both internally and externally? What kind of difficulties do you run into in this area?

All of our initiatives feature in the sustainability report and on the corporate site. They do not, however, reach the general public but people in the business, such as heads of sustainability and CSR in the multinationals, the world of NGOs and the institutions. The environmental initiatives are easier to communicate from the advertising and packaging point of view, whereas those concerning the supply chain and social aspects have to rely on indirect communication through our NGO partners. In general, in my experience, one of the most difficult channels of communications are sales points. This is especially true of in-store communication because there are many variables to be considered for correct, complete information on sustainability (although I know some companies such as Marks & Spencer in the United Kingdom are very keen on it). But sales outlet staff often only have asymmetric information since they have no access to the direct source of data. Moreover, there is a problem of frequent staff turnover, which means continuous internal training. I went to great lengths personally to try and find a solution and I spent a lot of time in shops working with salespersons trying to understand the tools, times and requirements… This confirmed my conviction that there is a great potential, independently of the average price and type of product. I must admit, however, that I only managed to share corporate information with staff in the retail division and no further, partly because within the company there were contrasting positions about whether this approach was suitable or not, for the reasons I just mentioned.

In short, how do you assess the role of a department like yours in the company? What level should it be situated at and to whom should it report? What are the prospects for the role of CSR manager and the development of corporate sustainability in general?

The CSR department is strategic for some things, such as managing the relationship with stakeholders. But we must remember that it should remain as streamlined as possible. You can facilitate the process, but we must avoid fuelling misunderstandings and passing the buck. In my experience, I know that where the CSR unit should be positioned within the company structure varies according to the features of the company and the way it has developed. For example, my department was made up of three different areas: supply chain, environment and community investments. When I joined Nike, they were all in a single department, which previously reported to legal affairs and then to marketing. As the corporate responsibility path gradually developed, new units were created to respond to the new needs, such as that for sustainable design. Around a year and a half ago, a gradual integration process was begun to merge some of the CSR units into the "classic" business administration departments and the subject of sustainability was gradually integrated into the business model. Similarly, the sustainable design unit has recently been absorbed into the main design department, CSR auditing has been taken over by financial auditing, and so on. This is an inverse process, but not backward. On the contrary, I'm convinced that when the path of sustainability reaches its mature phase this will be the normal situation: more than changing the things we do, it's a question of changing the way we do things, of relating internally and with the outside world. Basically, it's all about a change in outlook. You won't go forward if you don't have the sincere commitment of the company and the passion of the people involved. The company is a pragmatic organism that thinks in terms of opportunities. But to grasp the lasting opportunities offered by the development of sustainability you need so much transparency, honesty, authenticity and passion to succeed that it doesn't make sense to revert to old practices. There is no way back!

Carmina Campus: creating without destroying

Start-up and market position

Carmina Campus is a young brand that has gained an important position both in the fashion community and in the world of sustainability. Created in 2006, its first products were on the shelves for Christmas that same year. Its STOPFGM bags were sold by Massimo degli Effetti, one of the most interesting experimental fashion boutiques in Rome.

To understand the Carmina Campus vision we must go back to its origins and the culture of the product and of the work in the fashion world it comes from. The company founder, owner and designer, Ilaria Venturini Fendi was creative director of accessories in the Fendissime line and the designer for footwear per Fendi, until a few years after the Fendi brand had been acquired by the French group LVMH. This culture and tradition accounts for her special care over artisan aspects, the quality of workmanship and her deep knowledge of fashion business methods.

In addition to this traditional background, Ilaria Venturini Fendi is also very interested in the themes of sustainability, the environment and ethical working. "The idea of the STOPFGM (Female Genital Mutilations) came to me when I saw some canvas conference bags that AIDOS (an NGO concerned with women's rights) had created for a campaign against infibulations. Leftover from a few conferences, they were lying about unused and I thought I could modify them to make them smarter.

The idea was almost a game. Thanks to my background as a designer of high-end items, I could turn to Italian artisans whom I'd known for years and who had worked with me on some successful bags. Despite their initial perplexity because of the new features of such a different product, they agreed to work on these bags using the material – again recycled – that I suggested. The result was so encouraging that I thought a real project could grow out of the game, thus opening up a new field in fashion.

The first test in terms of public sales was a success. The bags sold quickly. The NGO benefitted and the product concept was immediately appreciated. And that's how Carmina Campus came into being."

The Carmina Campus approach to sustainability is far removed from the deliberately humble connotations typical of many initiatives in the field of fashion and clothing based on the ideas of critical or ethical consumption. The Carmina Campus bags and accessories are situated in the high price bracket and are sold in concept stores in Italy and in the main European capitals; they have featured in some mainstream fashion magazines.

The importance of transparency

The high-end price positioning was inevitable because of the large number of working hours required to make the bags. They are created by skilful artisans or communities involved in ethical fashion projects in a number of African countries, who are fairly rewarded for the true value of their work. Moreover, the craft nature of the processing and special material used mean that every product is one of a kind, thus justifying a high price in the eyes of consumers. In fact consumers can learn about the quantity of work involved in making the bags from the information supplied by an accompanying label: it details the number of hours involved in the design and production.

Indicating the number of hours of work required to produce the bag is a question of being transparent for the benefit of the consumer. We thus have a completely different approach to transparency compared to many large fashion brands which see it as potentially dangerous behaviour to be avoided because it would reveal marking up practices and the use of materials that are not exactly what consumers think they are getting. In the case of Carmina Campus, on the other hand, transparency is a key tool in showcasing products.

The Carmina Campus labels tell everything about how the product is made. In addition to the hours of work, divided between manufacturing and design, there is a detailed list of all the materials used in making a bag. They may often be of very different origin, ranging from shower curtains to computer keyboards, dustbin liners, embroidered table centrepieces, bottle tops and drawer handles. But in this case transparency is a way of promoting the product. In fact what makes the Carmina Campus bags so different and unique is their great variety and the fact they are made from recycled materials. Ilaria Venturini Fendi explains: "Every bag is almost a prototype. The research work and assembling is specific for each piece and sometimes we have to do a lot of tests on the materials before using them the right way, as well as to be sure the result will be excellent."

The label is thus an important way of communicating with the consumers and telling them exactly what they have bought. The labels, like the bags, are one of a kind. Customised and handwritten, they include the series number and information about the specific bag on which they are attached – like a kind of individual identity card.

Experimentation and fashion luxury business

Carmina Campus is positioned within the fashion luxury business, but in a very specific area, unlike anything else in the world of traditional glamour luxury brands and much nearer to experimental brands.

The fashion world still has to come to terms with the new awareness in consumers who are showing a growing interest in policies to reduce environmental impact, commitments to guaranteeing good working conditions and fair pay for workers, and the promotion of harmonious social development. The fact that few fashion brands, especially in the luxury segment have responded with conviction and passion to these new customer requirements is, according to Carmina Campus, due to a backwardness in the fashion business. It's as if the big brands have lost their relish for aesthetic and cultural research and are unable to keep up with the spirit of the times. In some cases, the new consumer awareness of environmental and social issues is perceived by the large brands but only interpreted as a kind of passing trend to be exploited and not as a cultural shift requiring a lasting change in production methods, aesthetics and corporate vision.

The Carmina Campus business model is centred on stylistic research and cultural sustainability. This strongly influences the choice of distribution and the forms the production process takes. The experimental features of the products mean they are marketed almost exclusively in a close circle of concept stores, like Massimo degli Effetti in Rome, 10 Corso Como in Milan, Dover Street Market, London, L'Eclaireur, Paris or the Isetan department store, Tokyo.

The organisation of the production process is also shaped by the features of stylistic research and the culture of sustainability, the principal focus being the exploration of the aesthetic and stylistic potential offered by reusing material. The process involves recovering material and combining various types, which are unusual and/or used in an innovative way that affects the production methods. All of this complicates the processing and requires an artisan approach: i.e. very high skills, great flexibility and a willingness to experiment with new methods. The poorer the initial material and the greater the various combinations, the more difficult it is to process that material and obtain top-quality results. This also means very careful selection of workshops and artisans as collaborators. There is a very close relationship between sustainable design research and craft and hand-working skills. The former cannot be done materially without the latter: design research and its material counterpart are inseparable.

Being part of the luxury fashion business inevitably means being involved with the fashion rituals and dates, as well as taking into account rapidly changing trends. Carmina Campus doesn't completely ignore the calendar dictating the rhythms of the fashion world. If for no other reason, because it determines the timing of the big stores' purchasing campaigns. But it's certainly not wholly dependent on it. New ideas and new projects develop from new materials as they are gradually discovered. The design process starts from a new idea or material and not from the need to rush out a seasonal collection to be presented at the main fashion shows and fairs. A new creative project is thus not developed in relation to a collection – the need to present new models every season – but within a family of products. And Carmina Campus works continuously on this family as long as there are reusable materials available. What counts are not collections but the continuous development of product families that have an enduring life that goes beyond the short-lived individual collection. Even the distinction between summer and winter bags is relative. Certainly some families of bags can have a seasonal feel. The "Shower Bags", made from shower curtains, for example, are more summerlike, but nonetheless are constantly presented, even when the fashion world is focused on winter. In short, these are lines or families of products – projects that don't dry up after one season. They are permanent products, although also continuously developed and mainly dependent on the availability of materials. The fact that in general the products are characterised as one of a kind or in a limited series makes it easier in practical terms to offer fast deliveries or deliveries between seasons. The sales opportunities therefore do not only come with the traditional fairs or fashion week events. Basically what attracts interest from shops are the original concepts, innovation, research and quality of the project rather than the fact that they might follow a seasonal trend. This commercial approach, moreover, is in line with the kind of distribution channels currently used by Carmina Campus – i.e. mainly concept stores – and would not be suitable for big chain department stores.

In recent years Carmina Campus has successfully taken part in events intended for a wider public of operators, such as the 2008 Pitti W_Woman Precollection, where the company was a special guest with its own dedicated space and event, and the Ethical Fashion events at AltaRoma in Rome. This kind of promotional activity is driving the future sales organisation towards a wider perspective, albeit within limits imposed by the identity of the company as an experimental brand.

Materials: reuse versus recycling

At Carmina Campus they like to be very clear on one point: what they are doing is reusing and not recycling material. The concept is underscored by the name of their flagship store in Rome: Re[f]use.

The materials used, or rather reused are scraps, dead stock and vintage material. They are not subject to any major revitalising work or physical or chemical treatment to "restore" them to an initial material state. So we are not dealing with recycling, a process in which the material is decomposed, reprocessed and given a new use in a different form from the original. In general, the energy benefits from recycling are not that obvious. Some materials require less energy to be produced anew. In any case they consume energy and although often efficient from the economic costs point of view, they are not efficient from the energy point of view. That is, they require more energy than virgin material would.

Reuse, on the other hand, involves no working on the material, i.e. all the material's energy is conserved without consuming any more. What changes in the case of the reuse materials at Carmina Campus are the context of use and the content of meaning. This is the outcome of an operation that involves exploring the aesthetic potential and significance of materials rather than doing opportunity-cost calculations.

Reusing existing scraps or material at the end of its life cycle in unpredictable forms and ways or the recovery of vintage components opens up new prospects for procuring materials that could also involve the consumer. What kick-starts the reuse design process is usually a hunch about the aesthetic and symbolic potential of the material. This is followed by contacts with the producers to see if there is any surplus, leftover or dead stock of the material in question. In other cases it may be the producer or user of the material looking for alternatives to the rubbish dump who asks Carmina Campus to explore its potential. After initial experiments on a reduced scale, today Carmina Campus looks for materials, stock and scraps in quantities that will enable them to produce on a larger scale. On the other hand, however, with extreme customisation and very limited numbers, Carmina Campus is beginning to explore the prospects of a relationship with materials that consumers themselves can suggest for reuse and so bring back to life old products in new forms.

Communications: glamour and sustainability

The fashion world, especially high-end products in the same price bracket as Carmina Campus, resort to conventional channels and forms of communication. At least until recently, they have given little room to sustainability. So being present in traditional communication circuits of fashion and at the same time supporting the values of sustainability characterising the brand means continuous experimentation in new languages and tools. Carmina Campus's first communications campaign was in leading fashion magazine *Vogue*. This was followed by appearances in many other mainstream publications, especially women's magazines, such as *Amica*, *Elle*, *Marie Claire* and the weekly supplements of the major Italian dailies. The values of "creating without destroying" and sustainability have been at the centre of various events featuring Carmina Campus. This was the case, for example, at the 2008 Pitti W-Woman Precollection and the first edition of *Lusso Esenziale* (Essential Luxury) at Macro Future, Rome, 2009. In 2010 Carmina Campus collaborated with Campari Italia on a limited series of 150 bags made by reusing PVC material from an installation by Ugo Nespolo entitled *Volta Campari* (Campari Vault) commissioned to celebrate the famous drink's 150th anniversary. More recently, the brand was at the first Treviso Festival of Sustainability, again in a dedicated space where, in collaboration with the fashion design degree course of the IUAV (Venice University Institute of Architecture), the company staged the exhibition *Save Waste from Waste*. The exhibition included a small selection of furniture made from reused material but most strikingly a collection of bags designed and produced from the idea that saving waste from waste was tantamount to thinking of a world in which much, if not everything, can be regenerated. The bags on show were made with large black doubled-up dustbin liners with a backing, usually made of leather. This gave them a consistency and wrinkled, worn look endowing the material with a completely new dignity and appeal. In 2011 as part of the Ethical Fashion at AltaRoma, the Re[f]use space hosted a discussion on entrepreneurship, green management and innovation, while in the White Room the bags from the African project were illustrated to a wider audience.

The initial Carmina Campus activities came from the idea of reusing canvas conference bags that had been abandoned as dead stock. The bags featured the logo and slogans of an NGO dedicated to the defence of women's rights in Africa. This was followed by a project called "Message Bags", which was implemented in Africa. Cooperation with woman in developing countries, again associated with the principle of reuse, is one of the elements that has been a feature of Carmina Campus from the outset.

Working in cooperation and sustainable development requires a very careful assessment of ideas and projects to be pursued since there are many attendant difficulties and risks. The African projects required a partner and so the company collaborates with the International Trade Centre (ITC), a joint UN and World Trade Organisation agency, in the Ethical Fashion Programme that the ITC had been pursuing in these countries. As part of the project, Italian artisans went to Africa to train people in the local communities to create a small collection of bags to be sold in the big supermarket chains. The bags are entirely produced in Kenya with locally collected recycled material. There are two models of shopping bags and the prototypes were specially created for the project: a square bag with a pleated bottom; and a smaller more vertical bag with an asymmetric rounded edge to make it easier to carry underarm. The more complex model was derived from the Carmina Campus Italian line called "Tetris" – small triangles of coloured textile inserted in the seam and some reversible bags which in the winter version are made of military tents and scraps of techno textiles from field or first-aid tents.

These models are "100 percent made in Africa" by the Kenyan communities. After training, the women in the communities use old safari tents and textiles from shelters for refugees. They add inserts of coloured textiles, usually offcuts from traditional local fabrics such as Maasai kangas and shukas (tartan cloaks and blankets). On one side of the bag are the words "Not Charity, Just Work", which sums up the philosophy of "Aid for Trade" inspiring the ITC. In addition to these 100 percent made in Africa models, the ITC projects also include the production of elements which will be included in more complex bags made in Italy. Like the "Message Bags", they have panels on which the women embroider freely chosen motifs and phrases. These bags were presented to the First Ladies in attendance at the G8 summit held in Aquila in 2009. The Kenyan women's contribution to the bags is not only manual work, but also creative and particularly significant, because they are free to choose the distinctive messages and designs.

The decision to create and produce in a sustainable way, to "create without destroying", cannot be limited to only one aspect, for example, that of protecting the environment through reuse. It is naturally also an attempt to improve the living conditions of all those involved.

Ilaria Venturini Fendi sums up the first few years of business at Carmina Campus: "This project has made me richer both in human terms and professionally. I'm learning a great deal and most importantly I've realised that there are various ways of being an entrepreneur. To those who work for Carmina Campus in Africa I say that if things go well for me they will go well for them, because it is a path that we are going down together and together we can grow."

SUSTAINABLE FASHION CONSUMERS HAVE GOT SOLAR PANELS AND DON'T HAVE SEX

Emanuela Mora, Marie-Cécile Cervellon and Lindsey Carey*

Introduction

What do Italians think about sustainable fashion and its consumers?
If seen in terms of a public opinion survey, this question is not particularly interesting. Passing moods recorded as reactions to multiple quizzes are little help in understanding if in overall Italian culture there is a growing trend among people to translate the values of sustainability into daily behaviour and attitudes. Moreover, for several reasons, the culture of sustainability seems to be encountering more difficulties in taking hold in the field of fashion. Fashion is by definition bound to the gratification of individual preferences, subject to rapidly changing trends (and consequently of the continuous replacement of used goods) and is produced through an extremely competitive industrial organisation based on the efficient economic exploitation of material resources and labour. The culture of sustainability, on the other hand, is interested in safeguarding the environment, protecting workers rights as collective assets and tends to oppose wasting resources and excessive consumerism. In the flow of meanings and continuously unfolding trends, sustainability means seeking a value that will endure over time. To begin, therefore, to understand in more interesting terms what Italians think about sustainable fashion, we need to ask another question: "What is the semantic universe of meanings and language in Italy today as regards the issue of sustainable fashion?".
There has been a rapid growth of interest in this fairly new topic over the last two years and consequently the spread of new languages, statements, projects,

programmes and information. Academics have now began to study this development and have produced some classifications in which various terms are often used interchangeably to indicate partially different phenomena.

Lise Skov, for example, speaking at the Modacult Conference in 2009, introduced the notion of fashion industry ethics to cover various areas: issues concerning the images of the male/female body as represented in fashion communications, the question of counterfeiting fashion products, animal rights and the more obvious rights of workers, protecting the environment and disposing of the large quantities of worn out or unused garments. Pretious and Love (2006), on the other hand, have charted the development of ethical codes of behaviour in sales people in the United Kingdom. It must be said that after the negative publicity surrounding big companies like Nike and Gap worldwide because of their failure to respect workers' rights and the environment, the theme of ethical standards has increasingly influenced consumers' perception of brands and sales channels. Newspapers, television and conferences have played a key role in constructing a shared view of the topics. But increasingly the most influential media as regards these processes is the Internet. With its capacity to host non-hierarchical comments and contributions from various sources and especially thanks to its interactive development (Web 2.0), the Internet has encouraged the creation of a language and common sense opinions that have spread widely, although at times not supported by adequate information. Although overall this book mainly deals with the latest technological and economic aspects of the theme, in the following pages we will try to describe the growing shared view of sustainable fashion, the everyday language used to describe it, the way in which people see the practice of consuming sustainable fashion and its leading players.

This chapter includes some notes in the margin to a small exploratory enquiry conducted on two fronts. In fact we searched the web to map out the way Italian sites deal with and speak about the topic. We also created two focus groups of ordinary consumers, chosen according to criteria of age and educational qualifications, to try and understand what they think about sustainable fashion, the space it occupies in the larger framework of overall fashion and who its followers are. The resultant picture is very interesting. It shows a wide-ranging and detailed semantic spectrum revealing the many varied issues that sustainability brings up when people try and imagine its practical applications to the field of fashion. We will also compared results obtained in Italy with those from a set of exploratory surveys in France and Canada. The creation of a set of comparative cross-border information is now a fundamental objective in assessing the potential development and spread of sustainable fashion, given that fashion by definition is a social, economic and cultural phenomena that goes beyond national borders with a global reach.

Figure 1 maps out the principal words and phrases used in web texts to speak about sustainable fashion. The map is based on four categories that define the semantic space in which most discourse on these subjects can be situated and that may be thought of as the extremes of two continuums. The first consists of the pair aesthetics versus ethics, the second of technology/market versus nature.

1.---

Map of principal words and phrases used to speak about sustainable fashion on Italian websites (copyright: Blumine and Modacult)

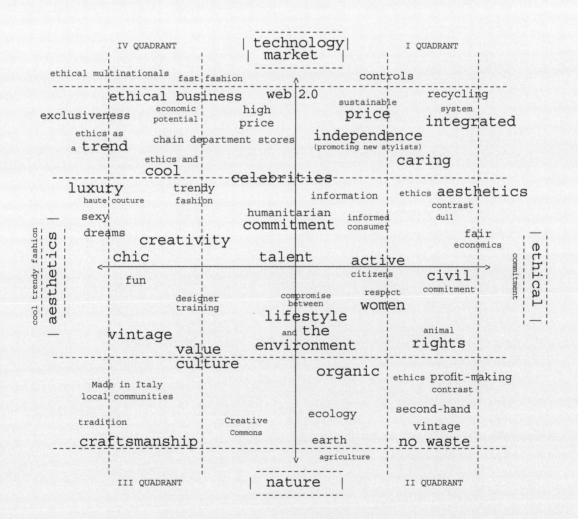

The contrast between ethics and aesthetics is deeply rooted in modern Western culture, which, although condemning the individualism and arbitrary judgements of an entirely aesthetical approach, exalts individual choices. At the same time, as far as ethics are concerned, any reference to a hierarchy of socially shared values is considered outmoded, although regret is expressed over the passing of a golden age (imaginary?) in which people were not forced to choose daily between an enormous quantity of consumer goods, modes of behaviour and lifestyles as happens today (Bauman 2000; Beck 2000). This contrast is one of the favourite themes in debates on fashion and its spread. On one hand, the continuous creation of new fashions has historically been justified as a response to the innate need for beauty and novelty that inspires modern men and women (Veblen 1999); on the other hand, however, the industrial production of fashion with its high aesthetic content and its brands endowed with the power of intangible seduction have led to semiotic saturation (Mora 2009). This has induced some sectors of the public to doubt the value added and promises made by many brands, which only seem to possess a purely commercial identity and have lost their capacity for aesthetic innovation. That's why more expert and sophisticated consumers make demands for moralisation and rationalisation, crystallised in requests concerning very varied aspects of the fashion supply chain: the reduction of the offering (and/or costs); respect of workers rights; the use of raw materials and production processes that are harmless to health and the environment; and the development of more efficient and sustainable organisational models.

The second contrast underlying our map expresses another pillar of the debate, that is the more directly internal issue of sustainability that distinguishes between the protection of nature and the environment, on one hand, and the application of innovative technologies to production processes and to market organisational models, on the other.

Sustainability per se is a very complex category and the subject of a great variety of often contrasting definitions. They range from the idea of sustainable development (which implies a socially governed approach to the capitalist economy) to that of environmental sustainability, often implying economic degrowth and at times a critical view of development and the use of new technologies in the name of a bucolic return to nature.

In conducting the survey we typed a number of keywords into the Google search engine, i.e. words used most often to talk about the themes we are interested in: ethical fashion, fair trade fashion, organic fashion, sustainable fashion, green fashion, ecological fashion, and eco-friendly fashion. For each hit with these words we considered the top 25 to 30 sites and so obtained a total of 300 sites for all the words or phrases. We were careful to select only sites in Italian. What kind of site did we find? Blogs, corporate sites, online newspaper archives, online magazines, portals dedicated to sustainability, portals dedicated to fashion, etc.

Given the variety of communications contexts, we found that the language was used for very different purposes: reports on social trends, tips for making purchases reflecting a certain kind of lifestyle, technical information about new products, raising awareness about non-profit organisations, advertising for various fashion collections, etc. Overall, however, these sites, together with many others that we did not consider, contribute to shared meanings around the theme of sustainability and sustainable fashion. They familiarise the general public with terms, concepts and images that become part of the vocabulary and stock of meanings in daily use. The effects on motivation and behaviour, however, have not yet been sufficiently investigated.

As Figure 1 shows, the map has four quadrants in which we have placed in a rational but arbitrary way labels that represent ideas about sustainable fashion found in the texts considered. These labels in most cases correspond to recurrent or key words in the texts. In some cases they were deliberately elaborated to sum up a more complex discourse.

Quadrants I and IV contain language revealing a deeper interest in technological innovation and ethics-aesthetics, respectively. By technological innovation we mean the complex semantic area that includes not only technology as applied directly to stages in the production processes but also to forms of organisational innovation and identifying new markets, i.e. new sections of the public interested in developing new sets of meanings and values (semiotic innovation). In short, in the area of technology we placed everything that implies man-made processes so as to emphasise the contrast with the area denominated "nature". The words and phrases in the first quadrant refer to all those processes that aim to protect nature and respect human and social rights through the application of measures with a high content of knowledge (certification, recycling techniques, etc.).

The idea that sustainable fashion may become an industrially and commercially important reality only if it has an integrated system, comparable to the traditional supply chain of design– production–sales in the clothing industry suggests that discourse on the subject has reached a mature stage and has come out of the more limited context of discussion begun in fair trade commercial (and consumption) circles and in political consumerism. Although obvious, we must not forget that those circles must be credited with having broken new ground by beginning to show how the end-consumer can influence decisions and strategies made in segments upstream in the supply chain (see, for example, the boycott movement called "Cleanclothescampaign", or the Milan fair "Fa la cosa giusta" ("Do the right thing"), which then spread to other Italian cities and regions (cf. www. cleanclothes.org and www. falacosagiusta.org).

It is a question of creating alliances between the producers: hand weavers who only make prototypes, artisans who make textiles on mechanised looms, and young stylists who wish to succeed in the field. This is the way to create a supply chain that produces competitive products, a bit like what happened in the organic food market.

(posted by a user on http://evabasile.blogspot.com/2009/11/moda-etica.html)

The topic of competitiveness combined with that of fair trade creates a peculiar and problematic cluster of meanings in the debate on sustainable fashion. On the map this is visible in the references to product prices and the importance attributed to information. In the first quadrant, it seems that the rationale of the integrated supply chain implies the need also to make the price sustainable as a way of justifying the whole process in the eyes of the consumer, informed about the value that each stage in the chain adds to the final product. This is the famous balance in the price-quality ratio, where quality is a very complex feature to define, since it includes not only materials, work and post-sales services but also measures environmental and social protection. Difficult to quantify and guarantee, they are of key importance in communications with the end-consumer. In the fourth quadrant, where the technological interest and market combine with a keen interest in aesthetics, the language is the same as that used in mainstream fashion: luxury, trend, dream, sensuality and exclusiveness. The price is a symbolic component, independent of the intrinsic features of the product and must be kept high to conserve product desirability. While in the first quadrant the focus of the language seems to be the relationship between more upstream segments of the supply chain with the end-consumer, considered to be informed and committed to playing a responsible role as a citizen, in the fourth quadrant, the focus is more on creativity as the driving force for all thinking about modern fashion, arising always from the efforts of those working in the planning and design stages, while the consumer is portrayed as waiting for readymade opportunities for fun and entertainment. In this view, sustainable fashion cannot become a business without the creative segments of the system involved in planning and communications. Here public discourse records one of the most interesting versions of sustainability, although arguably also ushers in confusion in the eyes of the consumer. In fact for some time now a number entrepreneurs and institutions have wondered about the real economic potential of sustainable fashion. Study centres, like the Centro di Firenze per la Moda Italiana (CFMI) and Modacult at the Università Cattolica, Milan, have organised conferences and publications on the theme (Lunghi and Montagnini 2007), while the big companies – from the luxury multinationals to fast fashion groups and the operators in the big chain department stores – have set up large-scale experiments (albeit limited to single product lines) in marketing sustainable clothing and accessories. The web mostly records these experiments without any great illusions. Sites simply document the attempts to do business without renouncing the criteria of aesthetics and sustainability.

I did a little search, obviously not exhaustive, and I was pleased to see that sustainable fashion exists, although in Italy it's struggling to get off the ground. In the last few years the situation has changed. There are several brands committed to this front, such as Muji, GStar, Levi's and Refuse to mention just a few.
(http://miranialepersonalshopper.wordpress.com/2010/06/21/abbigliamento-eco-friendly/)

An "eco-chic" current is now firmly established in the world of glamour and trends. The hope is that this, unlike what happened with other trends, will be longer lasting. Moreover, more than ten years ago one of the most famous names, Armani, launched his own eco-friendly line of jeans that were made using old clothes, jackets and skirts.
(http://www.acquistiverdi.it/content/view/1962/24/)

The [Italian] Coop has launched a fair trade textile line. It's called "Solidal" and has several different items of clothing from the South of the world: polo shirts, T-shirts, jeans, and shirts all made according to fair trade rules.
(http://www.acquistiverdi.it/content/view/1962/24/)

At present the most important sustainable material used by H&M is organic cotton. Organic cotton is made without using chemical pesticides and fertilisers, with obvious benefits for the environment and farmers. H&M has been selling garments made of organic cotton since 2004 and continues to invest in this material with the aim of increasing its use to 50 percent annually by 2013. Listen to the opinions of Henrik Lampa from H&M, Mathilda Tham from Beckmans College of Design and Marcus Bergman from the Swedish School of Textiles, Borås, on the subject of using organic cotton for sustainable fashion and you will discover what you can do to reduce your impact on the environment to a minimum.
(for further information on H&M's commitment to more environmentally friendly cotton, see www.hm.com)

Paradoxically, while the still fairly random marketing of sustainable collections and product lines by very different brands in terms of image, positioning and type of product highlights the fact that sustainable fashion is taking hold as an economic and social reality, it is bewildering for consumers, who struggle to understand what they are contributing to in terms of sustainability each time: the environment, workers' rights, development of poor countries, protecting Italian products, social responsibility, marketing strategy with no effective content, etc. People working in web communications, especially in interactive communications are obviously at the nerve centre of this confusion. But at the same time they are in a privileged position to monitor what is happening on the more innovative fronts as regards sustainability and to play an important organising and mediating role in the communications channels between all the stakeholders. As Figure 1 shows, in fact, the web is the key technological innovation in driving fashion culture from both the ethical and aesthetic points of view.

Quadrants II and III contain the language combining an interest in ethics and aesthetics with a strong concern for nature. Here we find talk about protecting consolidated markets, such as the top-quality "Made in Italy" markets (Quadrant III) and those more overtly linked to social and environmental protection (Quadrant II). In the second quadrant we included anti-capitalist and anti-consumerist language, which claim that ethics is incompatible with profit and condemns all forms of waste. Although understandable and shared by a significant part of the public, this language may be considered marginal, if we wish to explore the potential for the development of a sustainable fashion sector, which by definition must prefigure opportunities for profits and a process of replacing goods, even if on a different timescale to the dominant models in the textile and clothing industry. What requires closer examination in this quadrant are the various words and phrases concerning the rights at stake in sustainable fashion: from respecting the environment and the image of women (especially their bodies) to respecting the dignity of animals. Stripped of their fundamentalist component, these themes have entered the collective vocabulary and imagination concerning the sustainability of fashion. We have placed language about products "Made in Italy" in the third quadrant. In recent years this kind of discourse has primarily stressed the development of local artisan culture and traditions as a form of sustainability together with environmental and social sustainability. Traditions and emphasis on the local are found both in handing on knowledge and in the suitability of environmental and local conditions for certain specific textile productions. The excellence in craft working and respecting the cost of irreplaceable skills is also mentioned. In this initially apparently rather conservative picture, we actually find new ways of developing artisan creativity, including the use of new technologies, albeit to promote business models in which the potential for profit has not yet been clearly explored:

Cecilia, on the other hand, is the founder of the Pamoyo fashion brand, the first open source fashion label covered by a Creative Commons licence. The work is carried out locally by a group of young designers, and the paper patterns and designs are published online for non-commercial use in a blog that periodically reports on events and initiatives in the world of sustainable fashion. (http://noisymag.wordpress.com/200/07/08/fashion-reloaded-la-moda-open-source-a-berlino)

In conclusion, our rapid survey of the web has revealed how the language of sustainable fashion is now taking shape in the collective imagination, albeit in a still vague, fragmentary and fairly random way in the face of the strategies of individual companies that in various ways promote some form of sustainable fashion. The fact that the message does not reach the public in a clear way is evidenced by the discussion in the two focus groups of consumers, who, after having been asked to describe their relationship with fashion and consumer practices in the sector, were then invited to reflect on the theme of sustainable fashion and, lastly, to imagine identikits of sustainable fashion consumers.

Who buys sustainable fashion?

As the excerpts from the transcriptions of the focus groups illustrate (see below), the image of the typical sustainable fashion consumer has a number of clear-cut features and other fairly vague or even conflicting ones: she is certainly well educated and has the time and money to devote to shopping. Not beleaguered by everyday practical concerns, she's usually young, although not very, because she must be mature enough to appreciate the cultural values in sustainable products. In terms of socio-structural features, therefore, there are no doubts: money, culture and leisure seemed to be the necessary prerequisites to fill a consumer basket for goods that are considered costly, difficult and obscure. But in terms of character, affections and emotions, what kind of woman do we find? The profiles can be roughly reduced to two types: 1) a woman not interested in fashion, who takes no special care over the aesthetic dimension in her life; she devotes times to others and social life and takes a interest in environmental issues. 2) a woman who takes a good deal of care over herself, using many natural products and making very personal choices independently from the dictates of fashion imparted from above; she invents an original style. The first profile could be summed up as an environmentalist who doesn't smoke, drink or have sex. Many members of the focus group see her as a very drab image; the second is imagined as vegan, a bit hippy, red hair and freckles, who "suffers with plants".

She went to art high school... a young woman, around 30, or maybe she works at the fine arts school. Very straightforward manner, she doesn't dye her hair and takes no interest at all in aesthetics, no make up and so not showy, no frills, and no "Hello Kitty" – she knows nothing about those things, no frills and maybe at home she has solar panels, only eats organic and low-fat food, she may even be vegetarian and so doesn't drink, doesn't smoke and doesn't have sex. [Focus 2]

A person who is very fond of herself, because... if she makes eco-friendly choices she must in any case be interested in others and I think if you make that kind of choice you're very fond of yourself and then you pour this love that you have for yourself into others. I think she has a high self-esteem, so much so that she makes different choices, i.e. she doesn't follow the crowd, buying from Abercrombie doesn't matter, but she buys something anyway because she knows her action can help and can be an example; she thinks who knows, maybe I'll also influence my friends. A person who travels by train but is not necessarily sad. I imagine a very normal person, inquisitive who wants to make new discoveries; I don't know where she goes, but she goes by train; she is forward-looking with lots of friends, outgoing but begins from a well-defined self. [Focus 2]

I imagine somebody non-conventional, a bit hippy, into Hindu things because I see her as being in close contact with nature, she doesn't eat meat... you must surely be a vegan, she's very interested in nature and is a bit special. When she sees a plant dying she cries together with the plant. She's really into nature, someone isolated from the rest of the world... But it doesn't mean she's not interested. No, of course not! I imagine her physically as being tall, slender with carrot-red heir, quite pretty, a bit special with freckles, studied dowdiness, because she does have rather special clothes, but it's a very carefully studied neglected look. I think she's a very interesting person, obviously studied arts, over 20, she could even be a 60-year-old, I really have met 60-year-old women who are very extravagant and have an incredible charm. From 20 upwards. Because she must be fairly mature to behave in a certain way. I see her as being more adult, not a young woman; she must have had a lot of experience of life! [Focus 1]

Someone who has a lot of free time... a woman who doesn't work or doesn't work much, and at home she has someone who does everything for her, she's got cash confidence, definitely well-educated because she knows everything about the various certifications and so a person... who you can't make fun of. I associate being cultured with the fact that the more educated the person is, the more difficult it is to tease them, because they have a broader vision of the world but maybe it's not always that way; she's very interested in the environment and knows all about fabrics, etc.; she recognises all the certificates, she knows which organisations issue them; even those that are upstream in the processing, she's well-informed even about that aspect. [Focus 1]

N: I don't know, if somebody like that is careful about how she dresses, she must look after herself and be well turned out: i.e. if you have that kind of attention towards the outside world, you must also have it for yourself. So I don't know, she probably eats organic things. Age about 30, not very young and not even someone getting on in years. She must earn quite a bit but also have leisure time. Yes, she must earn a lot because these things are still expensive. Education – who knows! Probably something to do with ecology or about our planet in some way.
El: I agree that you need a certain open-mindedness, a certain sensitivity. I don't think that a woman working ten hours in a factory and struggling to make ends meet with only bills and children on her mind gives a dam about wasting Saturday afternoon hunting for an organic garment; in other words you need a kind of sensibility – let's call it that – and a certain standard of living.
N: Maybe she's a gardener, I don't know, I can imagine her in the midst of flowers.
El: ...And maybe even in a fairly sophisticated style, because I can't imagine her dressed in a simple way, with blouse and slacks, but I see her in sophisticated togs.
N: With her own particular style.
L: Not conformist, unconventional
M: Yes, and I can imagine this woman preparing her own makeup, like from powders. [Focus 1]

An international comparison

We find similar types of women to those just described in profiles resulting from cross-cultural survey conducted in France and Canada and involving in-depth interviews, focus groups and a survey of a non-probabilistic sample. The survey showed contrasts, however, between the typical green fashion consumer in the eyes of people interviewed in Europe ("a woman around 40, not sexy, with old-fashioned tastes, who follows a simple healthy lifestyle and is obsessed with environmental and activist issues") and her North American counterpart ("a woman around 20, sexy and interested in fashion, with an elegant personal style in line with contemporary urban living, confident, and expresses herself through her fashion choices) (Cervellon et al. 2010). How can we explain these rather extreme geographical differences? In searching for a possible answer we need to examine more closely the results obtained in France and Canada. In the two countries a total of 140 people were interviewed in 2009. The most striking result in the survey, in addition to the image of the typical sustainable fashion consumer is that the interest in sustainable fashion appears to be fairly limited, although it is a bit more pronounced in the Canadian respondents. Most importantly, the consumers clearly show a lack of knowledge and confidence about sustainable fashion products and brands. This pointed to the need for information campaigns on the nature of sustainable fashion and the certification processes providing guarantees. The main reasons why consumers bought a sustainable garment were, in order: an eco-friendly attitude, concern over issues of own or family's health, and ethical motivations. Moreover, the two national samples showed a peculiar difference: whereas the Canadians saw sustainable fashion as another aesthetic opportunity to express yourself and your own personality outside mainstream fashion, the French thought that it enabled people to express their social status in the latest form of trendy consumption. On an initial analysis of the results the differences between the two countries in how sustainable fashion and its consumers are perceived might be explained by the different target age groups of sustainable brands in France and Canada. In fact, in North America some green brands catering for a target group of young adults are popular. They have made social responsibility a very striking value in communications. Examples are American Apparel and Edun, a brand launched by the singer Bono and his wife. So in North America there are some very innovative, forward-looking brands which by addressing young people have chosen sustainability as a way of publicising their own fashion identity. In France, on the other hand, sustainable fashion is on the market mainly through brands associated with the fair trade world and political consumerism. In 2002 the Ethical Fashion Show, a major trade fair, was held in Paris. The event was attended by successful stylists with projects for social development and environmental protection. The political and moral component was proposed as an alternative to the glamour of mainstream fashion. In France, therefore, the world orbiting round sustainable fashion seems to cater more conservative sections of the population, albeit culturally "engaged". The businesses in this case express themselves through traditional channels such as fashion shows and show more interest in values fair trading than contemporariness. In Europe the theme of sustainability may have lost something of its edge because the public has grown tired of those organisations, such as environmentalist parties, who after a period of great visibility and vitality in the 1970s and 80s, are often seen as defenders of a conservative model rather than an innovative one and look to the past more than the future.

If we compare the international results with those obtained in the Italian survey, we note that, although the issue is very complex, we can map out the cultural spread of the phenomena we are studying today.

Firstly, it must be said that the organisation of a fashion system based on the strategic levers of sustainability is still at the embryo stage. In reply to the question what they thought sustainable fashion was, most participants in the focus groups associated it with fair trade and the commitment to organic materials or recycling of textiles and fibres. Only later, and especially when they were asked to provide an image of the typical consumer of sustainable fashion, some of them stressed that to develop such an active interest in the environment and towards others, consumers of sustainable fashion must be confident women with a high self-esteem. At a superficial level, therefore, the sustainable value of fashion would seem to lie in its ethical and prosocial character: i.e. especially an interest in the environment and workers' rights. The aesthetic value is acknowledged by those who see self-centred activity and self-care (i.e. health, well-being and independence) as part of prosocial behaviour. What is not said, but can be read between the lines, is that a woman who dresses "sustainably" is someone capable of resisting the lure of mainstream fashion (which most women do yield to) since she has no need to build up her confidence with brands and magazines. That the quest for a personal dress style goes with the behaviour and choices of an environmentalist and ethical type had already been confirmed in a sample enquiry on critical consumption of Italians conducted in 2005 (Mora 2007, pp. 90-93). The relationship between ethics and aesthetics is still difficult to pinpoint, partly because overtly sustainable collections are mostly judged to be rather plain by all the participants in our focus groups and even by those who think women dressing sustainably are potentially interesting.

A second element not to be neglected is the role played by the prices of sustainable garments. In much the same way as happens when talking about organic food or fair trade, garments labelled as sustainable are considered to be too pricey as regards value/quality.

As for the T-shirt that I bought, it had "organic cotton" printed on the fabric. It wasn't on the label but printed on the T-shirt. Then I noticed that it was a bit laddered like a knitted item, although I don't know if it was just that one in particular. [Focus 2]

Reading these comments – and some people interviewed were also aware of this – you get the impression that the information was incorrect, incomplete or confused and tended to lead to a misunderstanding of the phenomena being discussed. But where, on the other hand, reference is made to consolidated and clearly positioned brands in the pyramid of consumption, price is no longer a crucial variable in the opinions on sustainable products.

Recycled cotton... by Paul Smith, I don't know if you know the brand. I went to see the shop because they've got some men's T-shirts at the affordable price of 40-50 euros. So every now and then it could be a treat for a gift, and I actually bought organic cotton. [Focus 2]

At H&M there are things with a green label saying that they are made of cotton that blah, blah, blah and you say great and I don't know how but it's more or less the same price and so I thought great twice over. [Focus 1]

We might conclude that with a well-balanced supply – i.e. a justified price and an aesthetic value that is not exaggerated compared to mainstream trends – sustainable fashion should spread without running into major obstacles. Some studies have shown that consumers, even when they consider sustainability an added value, are not prepared to bear the burden of the cost of corporate social responsibility. The company is expected to work fairly and guarantee both ethics and aesthetics at the same price (Stanforth and Hauck 2010).

Seen together the studies carried out in the various countries confirms two interrelated results. On one hand, they suggest the ground to be cultivated in terms of the potential for developing the sector and, on the other, they indicate a limit to sustainable fashion (at least on a market unable to plan and organise its strategies for the long term).

The two interrelated elements concern the role played by the supply side in terms of demand and the widespread perception of incompetence and shortcomings that all the consumers interviewed shared as regards the knowledge they require to appreciate sustainable fashion. From all kinds of surveys and enquiries conducted on consumers and website contents, it emerges that the supply of sustainable fashion precedes demand and that the latter is rather uninformed and undifferentiated. Consumers are not very willing to discriminate between the various kinds of sustainability or to find out about the complex structure of the supply and distribution chain for clothing. So far the cultural image of sustainable fashion and its social, economic and ethical value has been produced by the companies and advertising agencies, usually not mainstream, on a market driven by entrepreneurs and professionals mainly pledged to fair trade and the environment. The definitions and distinctions between various kinds of sustainable fashion have still not reached mainstream fashion consumers (Mintel 2009). Consumers who for several years now have been considered sophisticated and environmentally aware are only such in the fields where a varied offering has encouraged the development of their capacity to choose and select. In the field of sustainable fashion, on the other hand, they have not yet begun to ask questions systematically, partly because information in the fashion world has never flowed easily and transparently. The system usually achieves a balance thanks to the way information about various aspects is jealously guarded: production processes, the creation of the style of different brands, and the length and segmentation of the supply chain. It is hardly surprising that consumers who participated in the focus groups felt rather bewildered. Most of the respondents in our focus groups, for example, believe they had incomplete information, because they had never received enough.

L: We're not very well informed.

F: Let's say if they're was an advert, a new logo publicising in this way [green marketing], I would certainly be attracted and I would go [to the shops], because I would like it. The problem is I haven't the foggiest idea where to turn to, I don't know where to find it [green fashion] apart from that drab stuff in the shops.

S: Yes but I think it would take an excellent advertising campaign with a big impact.

F: Like with the fur coats. It was pretty stupid but the animal activists did it and no one wears fur coats any more. My mother is ashamed to go out with one on.

G: Or give me the information. Tell me OK, you shouldn't buy this T-shirt. Buy this other one because anyway it costs one or two euros less i.e. you publicise the thing in a way that I can save some money and so I'm encouraged to look for given items, like organic garments, for example. I like them but there is no connection, in the sense that I eat an organic peach because it's better than the others but in fashion this hardly seems to be the case. [Focus 2]

Younger consumers have little faith in their own knowledge of materials and processes, whereas older ones, although mistrustful of the companies to give them sincere information about the processes used, still want the companies and the media to be responsible for informing consumers about how fashion products are made.

B: Of course there's no advertising and no information.

Mn: yes, not even in the fashion magazines.

L: No, there is no information at all.

Mr: Yes, yes they should already be talking about it in the magazines.

B. It should begin with marketing in newspapers, but also in *Non solo moda* [a TV fashion programme]. I've never heard anyone speaking about organic fashion or anything similar.

S: Yes, in the sense that *Vogue*, which is basically the fashion bible, should have a special section on it. [Focus 2]

One of the critical elements that the focus groups highlighted is the distance that the participants feel between themselves and their envisaged consumers of sustainable fashion. While sustainable fashion consumers are depicted as educated, independent, capable of creating a personal style, the participants see themselves as dependent on the images that fashion shows, magazines and companies provide; they are always in need of "brand confidence" and are uninformed about a universe of products and meanings that bewilders them, unless the information has the seal of approval of the official fashion world.

I find it hard to visualise [a sustainable fashion consumer] because I find it hard to believe that someone can only choose one kind of clothing, if it's not paraded a bit as fashion, as the latest fashion trend and, as you said earlier, the fashion of *paninari* ["sandwich-bar kids" – 1980s Milanese fashion for dressing with designer labels] at that time everybody bought those things, now its all eco-fashion and so everybody follows that; there is nothing special about her [the envisaged consumer] other than the fact she follows trends.

In conclusion, it appears that the time has come to raise some questions. What interests will attract the world of mainstream fashion to invest in sustainability to guarantee its own development in the coming decades? This question is crucial, because only if companies realise what is at stake will they also invest simultaneously in information and knowledge for the world of consumers. This information is necessary to raise awareness and the capacity to appreciate the value of a production model and of goods that have a complex content. At the same time we wonder if it is now inevitable that a top-down model of spreading innovation will persist in fashion, or if it is conceivable that consumer movements and the communicational and interactive potential offered by recent developments in the Internet will encourage greater independence for consumers and a capacity to put forward their own ideas. Lastly, we may also usefully ask if sustainable fashion is a development model suited to mature industrial systems with high labour costs and highly evolved legislation protecting the environment, or rather if it is not a model with global potential, now that new Eastern players are beginning to organise independently from the Western industrial systems. If this is the case, the theme of sustainable fashion will intensify with inevitable effects on consumers' images and perception of the phenomenon. Moreover, this will lead to better informed, innovative attitudes and expectations in the sector. At that point it will no longer be enough to have a supply based on the goodwill and commitment of a few active entrepreneurs and shopkeepers personally responsive to social and environmental issues.

* Emanuela Mora, Università Cattolica del Sacro Cuore, Milan; Marie-Cécile Cervellon, International University of Monaco; and Lindsey Carey, Glasgow Caledonian University.

Selected Bibliography

Th. Veblen, *The Theory of the Leisure Classes*, New York 1994 (original edn 1899).

Z. Bauman, *La solitudine del cittadino globale*, Milan 2000.

U. Beck, *I rischi della libertà. L'individuo nell'epoca della globalizzazione*, Bologna 2000.

M. Pretious and M. Love, "Sourcing Ethics and the Global Market", in *International Journal of Retail and Distribution Management*, 34, 12, 2006, pp. 892-903.

C. Lunghi and E. Montagnini, *La moda della responsabilità*, Milan 2007.

E. Mora, "L'abbigliamento tra etica ed estetica", in *La spesa responsabile. Il consumo biologico e solidale*, edited by E. Mora and L. Bovone, Rome 2007.

Mintel, *Ethical Clothing - UK 2009*, Mintel International Group Limited 2009.

E. Mora, *Fare moda. Esperienze di produzione e consumo*, Milan 2009.

M.-C. Cervellon, E. Hjerth, S. Ricard and L. Carey, "Green in fashion: an exploratory study of national differences in consumers' concern for eco fashion", 9th International Marketing Trends Conference, Venice, 21-23 January 2010.

N. Stanforth and W. Hauck, "The effects of ethical framing on consumer price perceptions", in *Journal of Fashion Marketing and Management*, 14, 4, 2010, pp. 615-623.

FROM THE FASHION FOR GREEN TO GREEN FASHION

Lucio Lamberti and Giuliano Noci*

Green marketing: the same old story?

Since the 1960s and 70s companies have been pursuing practices to highlight the green nature of their products and services. This was a response to growing public awareness about environmental themes. It was fuelled, on one hand, by deep social changes at the time and, on the other, by the emotive reaction to the first environmental catastrophes, to which a rather irresponsible development model had exposed humanity. In this context, companies began to consider the environmental performance of their products as value drivers and/or additional attributes able to make their offering more attractive. Some decided to speculate on the mainly emotive nature (especially after Chernobyl) of market sensitivity by offering products in which the claimed superiority of environmental performance was a surrogate for functional performances. In other words, companies proposed products that underperformed from the aesthetic or functional point of view but resorted to greener materials and technologies which justified the underperformance and at times exorbitant prices, since the market tended to reward environmental initiatives in any case. You only need think of the first reams of recycled paper. They were rougher, greyer and less easily handled than traditional paper. Although anything but attractive, they were "green" and as such commanded prices decidedly higher than average for the category. Obviously this approach based on the paradigm of "give less for more" could not last: it was founded (like many similar initiatives even developed in recent times) on a lower market sensitivity to price and (new and) significant sensitivity to environmental themes. In given historical moments, this triggered off viral phenomena that involved a significant number of customers and therefore companies who launched products described as being green. There was a bandwagon effect. But it then ground to a halt at the same speed as it had developed, once the outside drive to green ended, whether it had started as a media echo of environmental catastrophes, the effect of emulating testimonials, or something else. In other words, when the emotional element diminished, the rational aspect in the purchasing process always took over: i.e. the need to satisfy functional needs at the lowest price in a framework of acceptable collateral features – including environmental ones – of both product and supplier.

That is why so-called "green marketing", i.e. marketing products and services by emphasising the environmental performance, have swung from moments of great success (especially in the late 1980s when the topic was at its height in terms of media coverage) to moments of less interest when complementary phenomena exercised a greater appeal (for example, social and ethical issues, which took on a central role in the late 1990s).

So why should talk of green marketing today yield different results than in the past?

Are there any real reasons making it worthwhile eschewing very short term investments in order to concentrate on a long-term strategy aimed at improving environmental performance?

The answer is yes, and it can be divided into three points.

First, public awareness about the environment has changed. The themes of responsible consumption of resources, sustainable development and the repercussions that non-sustainable production and consumption can have on our lives and on the next generations have created a debate and an awareness about the green economy that affects political decision-makers, companies and civil society. In other words, the transitory and "wave-like" trend for environmental awareness is gradually being replaced by a deep rooted and strongly critical awareness that influences purchasing choices. We are experiencing a shift in the nature of environmental performance. It is no longer simply an advantage able to generate surplus value but a thoroughgoing customer requirement, i.e. a *condicio sine qua non* for the inclusion of a product among purchasing alternatives. A study by Mintel (2009) shows, for example, that 36 percent of American consumers declared that they regularly or always bought products with high environmental performances. In 2007 this figure was only 12 percent and so it is even more impressive considering that the United States are not even among those countries most responsive to environmental themes. Moreover, 2009 was the year of the biggest economic and consumption downturn in the last 80 years.

If buying green was only a passing fad, the crisis in consumption would have mainly affected the least indispensable purchases and should have led to a collapse in the green market. *The Consumer Environmental Survey 2009*, however, shows that the tendency to acquire green products during the crisis remained the same for 44 percent of American consumers who already bought green, whereas it only fell by 8 percent overall. A Deloitte survey reveals that today 63 percent of consumers deliberately look for products with high environmental performances when making their purchasing choices. The implication of this phenomenon for companies is self-evident: "The business model that sees green as a lever to exploit only for limited periods of time to obtain extra profits by riding the bandwagon will not grasp the opportunities for creating value offered by green marketing."

The second great change concerns technology. Today it enables companies to pursue improvements in the environmental performance of their products without diminishing the functional features on offer. Indeed environmental improvements in technology may bring improvements in products. Examples in this sense have come from IBM and Google in the field of IT. Through an action aimed at saving energy in its own servers, they provide their customers with the same functions at lower running costs. Similarly, through a systematic analysis of energy consumption in its shops and by redesigning its interior lighting, a leading brand in clothing like Marks & Spencer has combined energy savings and a green positioning with the development of more attractive sales outlets for its customers. These kinds of initiatives, moreover, not only demonstrate how an informed integration of environmental issues into corporate strategy may lead to innovation and the creation of stable competitive advantages. They also convey a strongly innovative message with wide-ranging effects: a green policy is not simply an additional element in the offering but an integral part and a driver of functional and symbolic values. If we then add that the systematic nature of green purchases and customers' desires to find a solution with high environmental performances lead to a greater attention to the price of green products, the consequence is both clear and revolutionary: "the 'getting less for a higher price' paradigm of green marketing is not only unsustainable in the long term but is always less effective in the short term."

The third great ongoing revolution, which will change the green marketing approach required to create value for the customer and the company, concerns more accessible and more diffuse information. In a context characterised by growing customer environmental awareness – revealed by greater interest in news about corporate environmental conduct and increasing participation in debates on themes associated with sustainable development – information and communication technology provide a far-reaching platform facilitating the spread of news and the sharing of opinions (as, for example, in social networking). These platforms create bonds between participants and tend to strengthen awareness about the issues dealt with, giving rise to particularly interesting phenomena that cannot be ignored by anyone wishing to implement a green marketing strategy. One of the most important examples of a forum in numerical terms is the TerraChoice project (terrachoice.com). On this community site, users discuss the practice of greenwashing: i.e. the corporate strategy of engaging in green marketing without the products offered and/or production process really having higher environmental performances. Through reports and contributions from tens of thousands of members, TerraChoice has not only contributed to the spread of awareness about greenwashing (basically not taken into consideration until the mid-1990s) but has also built up a considerable reputation thanks to denunciations and its provocative greenwashing awards periodically assigned to organisations guilty of the practice. These activities are given fairly wide coverage on the traditional media thus forcing companies engaging in greenwashing into costly communications, corporate social responsibility and redesigning production processes to recover their lost reputations. In this sense what emerges is a greater market focus on the solidity and strategic consistency between green positioning and corporate strategy, while the induced risk involved in greenwashing is highlighted. Hence "the pursuit of green marketing objectives requires an effective integration of green strategy into corporate strategy."

Why should fashion go green?

In the light of the situation just described the adoption of green practices is clearly a much more complex process for companies now than in the past. It is very interesting to see why the fashion industry, which compared to many other economic sectors (e.g. energy, automotive, information technology, etc.) comes under less pressure from regulators and customers, has so conspicuously and widely undertaken projects based on eco-friendly concepts. There are many reasons and they go far beyond an understandable spirit of emulation, i.e. imitating what has been done in other sectors, and/or the expectation of increasingly tough environmental regulations. They can in our opinion be attributed to four main reasons.

Firstly, the fact that green is fashionable suggests that fashion must go green. Such a widespread and important behavioural and cultural phenomenon as environmental awareness has inevitably affected the fashion world, in which interpreting market tastes and trends is vital. Moreover, in addition to being fashionable, the green dimension combines distinctive elements with often significant premium pricing. Clearly then, adopting a green approach can be very useful for a fashion brand's positioning objectives.

Secondly, the path towards green production is very interesting because the fashion world, especially textiles (and natural fibres)[1] can find leverage on the naturalness and sustainability of its own offering in a direct and easily understood way for the market compared to other sectors. One particularly interesting project in this sense is Sustainable Cotton (www.sustainablecotton.

org). This project aims to inform the markets on the environmental benefits of a low-impact cotton weaving and production chain by showing the savings in terms of CO_2 emissions, water consumption and land cultivated when consumers purchase eco-friendly cotton instead of industrial cotton.

Thirdly, adopting a green policy can enable fashion companies to develop innovative capacities and new value drivers. An emblematic example in this sense is the Swiss bag producer Freitag (`www.freitag.ch`). It launched a line of bags produced using only recycled materials (safety belts, pieces of truck tarpaulins, tyres, etc.). The result was a remarkably resistant product with a very distinctive offbeat style. This green positioning combined with original business ideas and some co-creative marketing initiatives led to premium pricing even when using low-cost materials (Freitag shoulder bags cost from 90 to 250 euros).

Lastly, we must stress how independently of the environmental issues, the fashion world has often been affected by ethical scandals (the most emblematic case has concerned Nike and the production of footballs in Asian factories employing underage workers), especially in remote production locations. Integrated into an overall management strategy of corporate social responsibility, a green policy is an interesting lever for establishing a distinctive international brand reputation.

Taken together these observations reveal that the fashion sector has great green development potential. Possible advantages from a strategic development in this direction may be very important and contribute to the growth, consolidation or revitalisation of companies in the sector. But understanding how these benefits can be obtained in practice is a different matter.

How should fashion go green?

Implementing a green marketing plan means: 1) satisfying customers' complex diverse needs through the promotion of practices, lifestyles and sustainable behaviour; and 2) guiding customers towards more responsible brands and forms of consumption. All of this comes in a context of a market increasingly interested in assessing a companies environmental performance and increasingly inclined to stigmatise greenwashing by boycotting products whose green claims fail to correspond to the reality of the company's practice.

To be successful, green marketing must thus be "embedded in corporate strategy": if a company is not green, if it's business strategy is not really aimed at improving environmental performance, green marketing cannot contribute to the creation of economic value. In line with this vision, John Grant (one of the leading living experts on the theme of environmental management) stresses how the success of green marketing depends on its being characterised by the so-called 5 Is. In his view, green marketing should be:

1. Intuitive. The green value and the environmental alternatives must be

conveyed in a simple way. The idea of a green market area as only for well-informed customers, "devoted" to green living, is the legacy of an outmoded conception of green marketing and fails to take into account the extent of the potential market or, at the same time, how increasingly difficult it is to attract the market's attention and interest.

2. Integrative. This refers to the need to demonstrate how environmental performance is not simply the result of a specific action on one product but the outcome of a programme of actions aimed at improving environmental performance in the entire production process.

3. Innovative. A company should have the capacity to create new products and new lifestyles through green marketing initiatives. One particularly interesting case from this point of view is Earth A'Wear (www.stepin.org). In this sustainability awareness project for the fashion world, innovations are aimed at demonstrating how eco-friendly fashion can be in the technical and stylistic forefront. The discussion touches on subjects such as the use of pineapple fibre in textiles, bicycle tyres in the production of belts and recycled materials in the production of biodegradable shopping bags.

4. Inviting. This means being able to attract customers by guaranteeing better performances compared to non-environmental solutions on the market.

5. Informed. In line with the vision of rewarding virtuous behaviour on the market (i.e. aimed at rewarding products\brands with higher environmental performances), green marketing initiatives must educate the market and raise awareness about the environmental impact of customers' purchases. From this point of view, it is interesting to note how one of the first online fashion product sales sites Yoox (www.yoox.it) launched the project called Yooxygen aimed at informing visitors (especially younger ones) about the environmental impact of producing clothes. Green marketing is no longer a question, therefore, of creating eco-friendly but underperforming products and the consequent implementation of advertising campaigns making environmental claims. Companies are asked to develop innovative and high-performing systems of offerings which by levering on lower environmental impact are able to convey a greater value (in terms of function, emotion or loyalty) to the market. Many levers are available for management to make a value proposition more inviting: reduction of environmental impacts associated with purchases and productions (e.g. through the use of recycled materials); development of quality products and superior design exploiting low impact production factors (for example, textiles obtained in an eco-sustainable way); extension of product life cycles, which thus reduce the rate of replacement due to wear; incentives for recycling processes, etc.

From the management point of view, companies are asked to rethink production and distribution processes, so as to develop at times even radical product innovations, and to integrate green marketing actions into corporate strategy.

The success of green marketing initiatives will be the logical consequence of a value proposition in which the environmental values of the product and the company are wholly consistent, thus making the proposition credible in the eyes of the market. The brand undoubtedly plays a crucial role not only as a distinctive factor of the product but also as a compendium of the functional, ethical and environmental values of the company. The definition of green marketing strategies and actions needs to start from an analysis of the meanings and values of the brand on the market, the kind of experience promised and the brand reputation. This analysis will highlight the strengths and problematic issues that the brand carries over into its approach to the green market, as well as the more strategic areas of action. For example, a brand associated with a strong image of innovation, or even with a reputation for being outrageous, will obtain more advantages from a green marketing campaign in which brand values are emphasised. This can be done through clamorous communication initiatives, resorting to testimonials well-known for their interest in environmental issues, launching non-conventional market initiatives, etc.

The greening of fashion

A successful green marketing project involves following a very complex path. A fashion company wishing to implement this kind of project must bear in mind some key elements.

Firstly, when adopting a green policy the need to strengthen a brand's responsiveness to the outside world must not be neglected. Environmental awareness, as we have said stressed, is refined and consolidated through relationships and dialogue between individuals. Internet, social networking and the contents generated by users are the true yardstick of the environmental awareness of the market. Companies must therefore develop processes and structures to monitor awareness, to dialogue with individual customers and groups and to convey messages informing about environmental issues.

The so-called Web 2.0 and information and communications technologies have been a crucial lever in this process. But we must not overlook the role of physical channels of distribution, as the case of Marks & Spencer demonstrates. Stores are still fundamental points of contact for communicating brand values and establishing a constructive dialogue with the market.

Secondly, we must stress how the importance of tuning into the public is based on the realisation that the debate on sustainable development translates into continuous changes in market expectations. A serious green marketing project must therefore guarantee the development of innovative capacities that not only generate short-term "virtuous" systems of offerings but are able to sustain the capacity of the company and the brand to meet the changing needs of the market.

In a medium-term perspective green products will tend to become normal commodities because of increasing competition on the green market and ever more sophisticated market demands. Therefore the pricing premium will tend to diminish (while non-green products and brands may even run into serious problems of legitimation on the market, basically in the same way as those companies that have been sullied by irresponsible conduct, see the dramatic case of British Petroleum). In this sense what becomes of key importance is the company's innovative capacity not only in terms of effectively differentiating the offering but also in terms of internal efficiency.

Because of their technical and management skills, human resources play a crucial part in the now key role of product and process innovation. Attracting excellent skills becomes a vital step on the path towards implementing a green marketing strategy for two reasons. First, it increases the probability of generating a successful green offering and triggers off a potentially virtuous circle: a company's eco-friendliness and the capacity to demonstrate it in practical terms to its stakeholders becomes increasingly important in assessing the attractiveness of a job, and therefore is a differential advantage in the competition for talent. The case of Google is emblematic in this sense (www. google.com\green). It set up a complex programme of green initiatives aimed at creating loyalty and attracting talents in the face of growing interest shown by the high potential IT world in Facebook. Second, attracting talents – they are usually increasingly sensitive to environmental issues – also enables companies to identify advanced green marketing and green management initiatives and so in turn consolidate their environmental positioning, thus closing the circle.

Overall we can say that the market for green products is an increasingly practical business opportunity for companies. The potential for the world of fashion is equally important. The challenge is far from simple. It involves not only marketing or production methods but a company's entire value chain and strategic market architecture. It is a challenge that must be met, however, to guarantee survival in the long term for companies and for the whole economic system. Green products are also a remarkable chance to introduce new competitive differentials in an international context that has shown how a growing trend to bigger volumes penalises high-quality innovative productions in favour of low-cost ones from emerging countries. That is why the greening of fashion is one of the most important levers in reshaping and ensuring the lasting worldwide success of products made in Italy and/or Italian style.

*Department of Management Engineering, Politecnico di Milano

[1]There is a lively ongoing debate about the environmental impact of growing linen and cotton. Farmers argue that water consumption in growing natural fibres and the level of CO_2 emissions is much lower than in the production of synthetic fibres (usually derived from fossil fuel), while environmentalist associations wish to promote the production of organic fibres. From this point of view, they accuse conventional farmers of being the main users of fungicidal and pesticide chemicals worldwide. The intensity of the debate is emblematic of the attention that the environmental issue raises even in sectors not considered to be of high environmental impact.

FOUR.
POLICIES, OBJECTIVES AND TOOLS FOR SUSTAINABLE FASHION

SUSTAINABILITY AND THE FUTURE OF THE ITALIAN FASHION INDUSTRY

Marco Ricchetti

The ailing Italian fashion industry

For around five years now the Italian fashion industry has suffered from a widespread malaise, only slightly mitigated by the success of its more innovative brands and the permanent strength of its historic brands. The difficulties, moreover, are evidenced by the fact that even some big names have succumbed. The malaise cannot be entirely attributed to the sweeping trade liberalisation from 2005 to 2008, which removed all barriers to imports into Europe and the United States. Restrictions to the international trade system of textile products and clothing had been introduced by the 1974 Multifibre Agreement, later modified by the WTO Agreement on Textiles and Clothing (ATC). Nor can the difficulties be wholly blamed on the financial downturn that shook the international markets in 2008-2009.

These were certainly two important shocks, especially liberalisation, since it brought Italian companies face to face with fierce competition and coincided with China's eruption onto the scene as a key world player. The shocks partly explain the malaise in the Italian fashion system but are not sufficient to explain its gravity. In the early 2000s, the Italian fashion industry had actually managed to come off strengthened from a difficult restructuring stage, partly helped by the rising price of the euro. On the eve of international trade liberalisation it was thus in a better condition than many observers had feared. Similarly, at the height of the financial downturn, it was ready to benefit from the first signals of recovery.

Consumption in Italy from 1972 to the present

Total consumption and clothing

```
+91%
  Λ
  ¦         ----clothing
  ¦
  ¦         ----total consumption
  ¦
 +50%
  Λ
  ¦
  ¦
  ¦        +26%
  ¦  +22%   Λ
  ¦   Λ     ¦              +17%
  ¦   ¦     ¦      +18%    Λ
  ¦   ¦     ¦       Λ  +4% ¦          +0.4%
  ¦   ¦     ¦ -0%   ¦   Λ  ¦     -4%   Λ
  ¦   ¦     ¦       ¦   ¦  ¦      V
──┴───┴─────┴───────┴───┴──┴──────V────┴────────
 1970-      1984-    1994-   1994-     2004-
 1980       1994     2011    2004      2011
```

Source ISTAT

The missing element in the explanation must be sought in the stage before trade liberalisation and the financial crisis. In fact its origins lie in the changing models and consumer trends of the late 1990s, a period that was still favourable to the Italian fashion industry. The successful Italian fashion model had developed and prospered at the time of fast growth in consumption. Purchases of clothing rose either more than average (as in the 1970s and early 1980s) or were in line with general consumption (as in the 1980s and early 1990s). Italian companies showed their flair at interpreting the consumption model and the spirit of the time by combining creativity, design and manufacturing skills much better than companies in other countries with a tradition for clothing and fashion industries, such as France, the United Kingdom or Germany. The features of that fashion consumption model dominated by status, image and conspicuous consumption are well-known. They are summed up by Francesco Morace in this book: "the fashion world created and adopted a very powerful model of relations with the market. It was based on inventing images and dreams rather than referring to real production processes."
In the second half of the 1990s the consumption growth rate fell drastically. This was due to a complex set of macroeconomic, social and cultural factors. Fashion consumption ground to a halt with no growth (0%) in the last fifteen

years (at constant price) and therefore at a much lower rate than average growth (+18%). The crisis in clothing consumption was accentuated especially after 2004, when consumption fell by four percent in five years. The crisis, or rather the lack of growth in consumption, translated into more selective behaviour by consumers who exercised greater care in choosing products and seeking value for money. The change cannot simply be directly attributed either to more critical attitudes to consumerism or a desire to save on waste. It was, as we said, the result of a complex set of economic factors concerning income and cultural factors that undermined the powers of seductive images and novelty. This form of novelty, moreover, was independent of the effective material contents of the product. In short, consumers were thus also less willing to pay high prices to satisfy the desire for fashion contents and novelty.

This behaviour involved greater selectiveness in purchasing and the phenomenon of trading up and trading down, described by Michael Silverstein and Neil Fiske in their bestselling *Trading Up: The New American Luxury* (2003). According to the two Boston Consulting Group experts, the bulk of consumers, i.e. those belonging to the middle classes, were willing to acquire some goods in a higher price bracket than they were accustomed to doing for their other purchases, i.e. they traded up for a select set of particularly important goods. These goods usually have a strong emotional aspect. However, before consumers will pay a higher price, the products must not only have aesthetic and symbolic values but guarantee or more simply demonstrate they genuinely perform better due to their material contents.

For the remaining products, those that consumers consider insignificant and for which there is no emotional involvement or high performance, we find trading down to the lowest price possible to save as much as possible and so also to fund trading up for other goods.

In this context – in which also for goods with a greater emotional involvement, such as fashion items, functional and material factors acquired a greater value than in the past – a new set of values came into being, the values of sustainability: i.e. sustainable environmental and social values that take on an importance that goes beyond the limited circles of ideological anti-consumerism and critical consumption to include broad sections of consumers in search of individual but also collective well-being. The new values of sustainability allude to material elements such as how a product is produced, the environmental impact of the manufacturing process, the effects on health from the materials and components in the product, etc. But they also allude to emotional factors: I'm behaving in the right way, I'm contributing to collective well-being, I'm making a rational choice, etc. These values fit perfectly into the framework of the new consumption model and are at times even "cool" and in line with the spirit of the times. Whatever the causes, the new consumer behaviours took over those that dominated the scene in the late 1980s and the 1990s. Among the consequences of the change was the demand for new forms of relations between fashion brands and consumers, to embody the new values and new priorities.

In other words, shifts in the culture of consumption undermined the effectiveness of the model based on images and dreams rather than real production processes. This model had been the guiding light for many Italian fashion companies during the golden years of success. To construct a vision for the future of Italian fashion and to pull it out of the straits of a now prolonged malaise, the issue of the change in consumer models must be tackled to bring fashion brands into line with the new spirit of the times, of which sustainability is an integral part.

Three alternative responses

Responding to the consumer changes is a key issue and will point to possible positive developments in the Italian fashion industry, or its decline. As we will see, it is strictly linked to the theme of sustainability.

We can outline three models adopted by fashion businesses to respond to the changes in consumption models. They have various points of contact with the history and features of the Italian industry and are three possible ways out of the current state of malaise. Obviously, the whole Italian system fashion should not necessarily embrace only one of them. The three models are not clear-cut alternatives but can coexist. Each may account for significant quotas in the industry.

Fast fashion. Fast fashion has probably been the most successful formula in European fashion since the late 1990s. It is very simple. Are consumers now less inclined to pay high prices for impulsive purchases only for the sake of fashion novelty? If so, the answer is to offer them new items always in line with the latest trends but at very low prices. Fashion at knockdown prices (or "reasonable prices" as one Zara slogan ran a few years ago) has also been scornfully criticised as "McFashion" (see, for example, Michelle Lee, *Fashion Victim: Our Love-Hate Relationship with Dressing, Shopping and the Cost of Style*, 2003; the term, however, had already been coined by a *Newsweek* journalist in 1983). Fast fashion has taken the pace of changing trends to an extreme by making the latest fad cheap.

The underlying idea of fast fashion is to increase volumes and slash prices. In countries like the United Kingdom, where there was already a culture of cheap clothing, the effect was revolutionary in dimension. According to a Cambridge Institute of Manufacturing study (*Well-dressed? The Present and Future Sustainability of Clothing and Textiles in the United Kingdom*, 2006), in only four years, from 2000 to 2004, the number of garments purchased per capita in the UK rose by over a third, partly thanks to a drop in per-unit prices of over fifteen percent. The fast solution mainly attracts trading down and therefore leads to more banal and lower quality fashion content in garments, although fashion is still the driving force in consumers' purchasing choices. Moreover, there is clearly a contrast between this model and the growing value of sustainability in consumer culture. The Cambridge Institute of Manufacturing study estimated that the effect of the rise in garments consumed, associated with the development of fast fashion from 2000 to 2004, implied an increase in the volume of waste of around 300,000 tonnes per year, at an optimistic assessment. Moreover, speeding up the rate of output and the pressure to cut costs threaten to create worse conditions and lower pay for workshops supplying the fast fashion brands. This means a growth in "grey" labour markets which, although not necessarily, may slide into illegality or irregularity, as a good deal of evidence seems to suggest. In Italy, for example, see the case of the Chinese district at Prato, specialised in T-shirts (Silvia Pieraccini, *L'Assedio Cinese – Il distretto del pronto moda di Prato*, Milan 2008).

Business as usual but on the emerging markets. A second possible response is to maintain the successful Italian fashion model of the 1980s and 90s basically intact or with only a few changes. If the observations on the changes in consumption models are correct, this approach will not guarantee stable growth in the next few years on the traditional Italian fashion markets, i.e. mainly Europe. It will thus require geographical diversification to reach the emerging BRIC markets (Brazil, Russia, India and China), for example, and their new luxury consumers, who today show behaviour and preferences not unlike – or even more accentuated than – those that characterised the Western markets in the late 1980s and early 1990s.

Moreover, no matter what competitive model the Italian fashion industry adopts in the coming years, there will be an inevitable and necessary change from mainly Eurocentric exports to more worldwide trends. Firstly, because independently of the consumption model, keeping exports focused on only one stagnant market, like that of clothes in Europe, is a very serious limit.

The main question about the post-financial crisis scenario will concern the growth prospects for consumption in the advanced economies and, especially, in Europe, where consumption has been stagnant for some time. Now fiscal policy restrictions, due to the stringent restraints introduced to rebalance public finances of all member countries, suggest there will be no significant growth in the next few years. In the BRIC economies, on the other hand, high rates of growth in consumption are forecast, along the lines of the trends recorded in recent years.

In the past decade household consumption in the BRIC economies have tripled and their increase in absolute terms has been greater than that generated overall by European families. A recent Goldman Sachs estimate shows that in the next decade the trends will continue in much the same way and by 2020 the level of consumption in the BRICs will be equal to that of the 27 European Union countries. Growth in the BRIC markets will not only be quantitative. The demand for quality will also rise and we can expect strong drives to innovation on that account. In the coming years, the market will move to these countries and, consequently, new opportunities will arise in them.

Italian companies have followed this line actively in recent years in Russia – the main element of novelty in the geographical structure of fashion exports in the last decade – and in China, while longer timescales are envisaged for the incipient markets in India and Brazil.

The development of the Russian market brought great benefits to Italian businesses but the BRICs also entailed some far from insignificant difficulties and problems.

The first is that the potential of these markets is in fact still only potential and has yet to be fully developed. Today the BRIC economies only account for seven percent of Italian fashion exports, even though they have tripled, compared to the very modest figures a decade ago. Moreover, this is in line with growth in consumption in those countries.

The second difficulty concerns the size limits of most Italian businesses. They are more suited to catering for nearby business cultures that are similar and have well-proven distribution systems. To fulfil the promises of profits, for example, entry onto big markets like China and India require partnerships with local operators and distributors, which are often several times larger than the Italian firms and want very big production quantities. Both conditions often mean that Italian businesses are simply not big enough. Lastly, we must not forget that the market and consumption models in emerging countries are evolving very rapidly and tend to align – at least in the high end – with trends in Western countries, especially as regards sustainability. In China, for example, although there is no widespread awareness among consumers, the issue of sustainability is already at the centre of public debate.

Sustainable fashion. The third possible response is to adjust to the evolution of consumption models and gradually adopt the culture and principles of sustainability as a driver of innovation and growth.

The fashion world is not considered to be among those particularly interested in the topic of sustainability. In many ways it is at the opposite end of the spectrum from responsible, sustainable consumption. There are strong reasons rooted in the DNA of fashion, which is frivolous, fickle and governed by the genes of originality, making the relationship of its businesses with the values of sustainability much more laborious. Indeed many observers believe the expression "sustainable fashion" to be an oxymoron. This vision of the fashion business is justified by some of its typical features, such as the sequence of fashion seasons that boosts consumption needs and then in only a few months makes garments obsolete and unusable, when they are still perfectly functional, or the stress on originality instead of usefulness, sustainability, etc. Yet fashion has not completely ignored the culture of sustainability. As we said, fashion mirrors what goes on in society and there are several examples of green brands and designers even in the 1990s (see, for example Lynda Grose with Esprit or Yvon Chouinard and the creation of Patagonia in the United States, while in Europe Katharine Hamnett had already presented her manifesto garments in 1985 collections). But until recently the fashion world as a whole has tended to fight shy and in some ways defend against green developments. What makes the difference today and has led to the need for fashion to change up a gear is that, unlike at the end of the 20th century, the values of sustainability have demolished the barriers between the notion of an aware, responsible consumer and that of the average consumer.

One consequence is that sustainability per se is no longer enough for consumers. It is an important attribute but it now must be combined with style and aesthetics. Sustainability alone will not make a crucial difference in consumer choices. It is not enough for a textile to be made of low impact natural fibre if it does not also look good. The conditions are now in place so that the pairing of the terms "sustainable" and "fashion" will no longer be considered an oxymoron but harmonious concepts corresponding to another rhetorical figure, that of the hendiadys, as in the title of this book: "the beautiful and the good".

A simple test to measure the popularity of the two terms sustainable and fashion used together can be conducting by resorting to the Google Trends web facility. It will indicate the volume of searches for paired terms on the Google search engine since 2004. We chose to use the English language since there is larger overall search volume and so the results are more significant. But instead of using the word "sustainable" we paired eco with fashion. Although its meaning is narrower, the phrase is more widely used by non-specialists. The results obtained using the pairing "green fashion" are only a little different, but there may be some interference due to the possible use of green in its literal meaning as a colour. The results of the analysis show that until mid-2007, the search volume in Google for the couple "eco-fashion" was too low to be reflected on a graph. But then by the end of that year the frequency was significant with peaks in 2010 (for the features of the algorithm that calculates the frequencies see: http://www.google.com/intl/en/trends/about.html).

The presence of the terms eco and fashion in searches on Google (analysis conducted in December 2010)

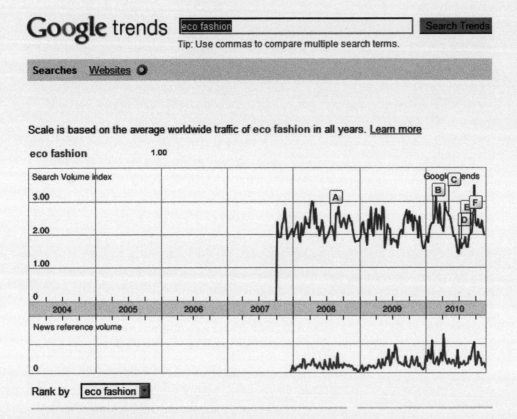

Source: Google Trends

Albeit with due caution, if we link consumer interest to the volume of searches on Google, we can surmise, if nothing else, that the original contradictory nature of the two terms has been attenuated.

Describing the values that the expression "eco fashion" has for consumers is a very complex operation and much work has yet to be done. Initial steps have been made in some chapters of this book. We run into difficulties in defining both terms. As far as the term "fashion" is concerned, we may ask how much its meaning is affected by the slowing down of the pace of change (on the contrast between fashion and style, see for example the arguments of the English anthropologist Ted Polhemus with reference to youth subcultures:

www.tedpolhemus.com/main_concept1%20467.html) and the revival of
the importance of material components. As far as the term sustainability
is concerned, its polysemantic nature generates a wide range of very varied
meanings for consumers.

We can attempt to assess if the connotations of the Italian fashion industry are
in line or contrast with the principles of sustainable fashion. An initial analysis
reveals that there are some factors of affinity.

Let us consider at least three of them:

The supply chain: sustainability is holistic in nature. A product is not more
or less sustainable according to the process in only one production stage.
Sustainability refers to the entire product life cycle, from the production of raw
materials to the end of the product's life. The traditional supply chain approach
once typical of the Italian fashion industry is thus a good starting point that
can be extended also to the stages of the production of natural raw materials,
distribution, use and maintenance of garments and their possible reuse. A
response to the change in consumer model that makes sustainability of central
importance would be an excellent opportunity for the Italian industry to re-
establish the special supply chain relations that characterised it in the past and
to link up the stages in the production cycle again.

Craft skills: as we said, sustainable fashion involves a greater stress on material
components, as has been illustrated in this book. Here too there are strong
affinities with Italian fashion's history and business model. Its distinctive skills
are found along the craft-design axis, the latter being solidly anchored to the
former. Mario Boselli has summed up this model with the expression "beautiful
and well made". This distinguishes the Italian model from other national
models which have emphasised communications, the brand and the distribution
networks – see, for example, the big French luxury brands and the American
distribution chains.

Local systems: the history of the textile, clothing, leather and shoes industry
in Italy was based on the system of the so-called industrial "districts". Over
time this model has undergone radical transformations and has arguably lost
part of its competitive strength. In any case it forged relations between all
the stakeholders – between entrepreneurs and unions, local communities.
The integration and involvement of all those who are affected by companies'
activities and in turn can influence them is a key tool in developing a
sustainable approach.

At least on an initial analysis, the solution in the direction of sustainable
fashion seems to have various elements in keeping with the culture and
organisation of the Italian industrial model. This suggests that Italian fashion
businesses might enjoy a competitive advantage over companies in other
industrial systems both in emerging countries and in newly industrialised

countries. Taking this direction may be the way out of the malaise we discussed at the beginning of this chapter.

If sustainable fashion is to develop strongly beyond the current isolated efforts or niche markets, it must overcome a number of obstacles.

The first fundamental obstacle is the absence of a system of clear and easily interpreted regulations enabling consumers to assess the degree of sustainability of products and to distinguish between companies making real progress on sustainability from those indulging in greenwashing (on greenwashing, see Lucio Lamberti and Giuliano Noci in this book, pp. 112). Transparency is a fundamental requisite if the market is to develop and if supply is to meet demand. The system of certification of sustainability is still generally complex and incomplete (on certification, see Lodovico Jucker in this book, pp 145-158), especially as regards fashion industry products and processes. To this we must add a specific difficulty intrinsic to the fast changing fashion world with its very great variety of products, making the process of certification complex and at times uncertain.

A second shortcoming that favours greenwashing practices and penalises businesses investing in sustainability concerns the sustainability claims made by businesses about the eco-credentials of their own products and processes in the absence of shared and enforced regulations.

In this case too, as in certification for products and processes, there are already at least three benchmarks:

- *The International Chamber of Commerce Code of Advertising and Marketing Communication Practice* (2006) is the most authoritative standard for the advertising world for the institutions and authorities regulating trade. In January 2010 the ICC published a specific proposal to supplement and modify the original code containing not only general principles concerning sustainability claims but also a checklist to assess them.

- Some recently published documents by the British government such as the guide entitled *Making a Good Green Claim* and *The Green Claims Code* in 2000.

- The US federal Trade Commission's *Guide for the Use of Environmental Marketing Claims,* currently being updated.

A good deal of work, however, has still to be done to define clearly how these principles can be applied to the complex world of fashion.

Lastly, one element concerns companies' behaviour rather than regulations.

At the last annual conference in the "Beyond Green" series (Amsterdam, December 2010), the conference moderator, James Weenhoff opened proceedings by saying: "sustainability can be a bit boring".

As we stressed above, reconciling sustainability and fashion will only be possible if we salvage in a sustainable key the aesthetic and creative dimension

that Italian manufacturers once successfully built into their products.
We may surmise that in a distant future – but perhaps not so very remote –
manufacturing and selling products sustainably and contributing to social and
environmental equilibrium will be routine for companies and brands currently
required to emphasise these aspects. At that point the focus will once again be
exclusively on the beautiful.

LOCAL CULTURES AND SUPPLY CHAINS. BUILDING A NEW ECONOMIC MODEL FOR FASHION

Giampiero Maracchi*

Globalisation and its economic model

The worldwide changes to climate and the environment must be seen in relation to the economic model of heavy industrialisation which reached a peak of expansion in the second half of the 20th century. The model was based primarily on the consumption of energy, which in the last thirty years has more than doubled (Figure 1).

1.--

A) Worldwide demand for primary energy.
Oil, gas and carbon will reach 83 percent of the total by 2030
(Source: elaboration of IEA data, World Energy Outlook)

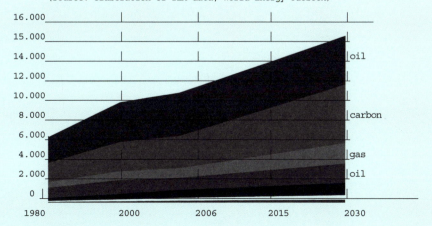

B) Emissions by sector

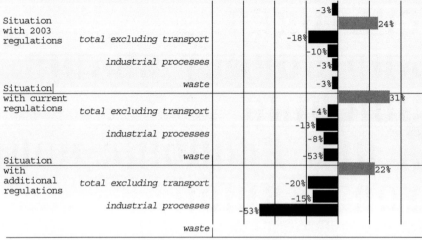

(Source: our elaboration of IEA data, World Energy Outlook)

The rise in energy consumption is mainly due to the entry onto the stage of industrial production of big countries like China, India and Brazil and to the fact that trade globalisation has increased the long-distance transport of people and goods (Figure 2), which has doubled compared to the 1970s. The increase in the energy consumption is directly correlated to the increase in climate-altering gases, which rose by 25 percent in the same period, with the well-known consequences for the global climate.

2.--

Energy consumption by type of end-use in OECD countries

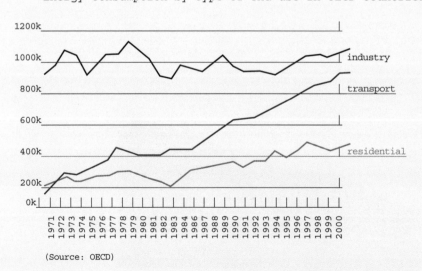

(Source: OECD)

Moreover, the rise in energy consumption underlies the gradual increase in economic indicators and especially GDP, which has doubled since 1970, as have other indicators but without the overall quality of life improving. Indeed quality of life has fallen rapidly since the 1970s, if we consider other indicators than the GDP, such as the Genuine Progress Indicator (GPI), which not only takes into account strictly economic aspects but also other aspects of the human condition (Figure 3).

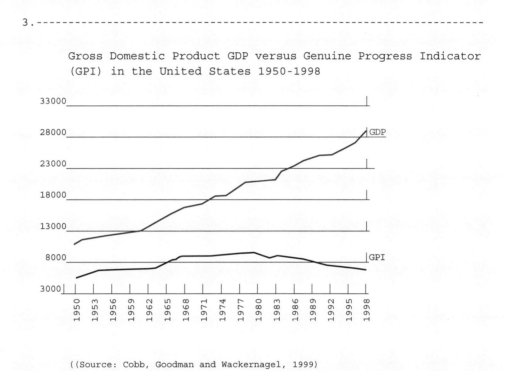

3.---

Gross Domestic Product GDP versus Genuine Progress Indicator (GPI) in the United States 1950-1998

((Source: Cobb, Goodman and Wackernagel, 1999)

These data suggest that consumption on the market beyond a certain threshold no longer improves the human condition but rather impoverishes it by creating serious damage to the environment. The liberal model in politics and free-market economics have brought undoubted benefits, such as reducing starvation, physical labour, many diseases and illiteracy. They have encouraged civil participation and civil freedom and have thus improved living conditions in industrialised countries. But they no longer enable humanity to progress because they are based on the patently false assumption that natural resources are unlimited.

As happened in the Renaissance, when philosophers, artists, statesmen and scientists developed a line of thinking that a century later triggered off the scientific, technological, industrial and political revolution, we must think about how to construct a new society in which the acquisitions of the last few centuries are consolidated. In this way we can reduce the negative impacts and resolve the glaring contradictions created by market methods blind to values and often also to common sense. You only need think of the sums of money paid to footballers and actors, completely out of keeping with their social value and inducing the poor in spirit to entertain false ideas about the scale of values to be emulated and to be used in educating the next generations.

On the other hand, human nature is characterised by great flexibility. This explains its capacity to construct scales of values and models of behaviour completely different from one epoch to another. The predominance of economic values in the 20th-century and the attendant social struggles, as well as the measuring of personal success only according to economic criteria led to many other aspects of life being overlooked. Today they are re-emerging as a response to the overall general crisis in the economic and political system.

For a better understanding of the 20th-century phenomena, we must outline the main features of the current economic model, based on industrial production increasingly concentrated in the hands of a few groups operating in many countries. More and more often they make decisions independently of political power and local social control. This concentration in a few groups also applies to the banking and financial sector. Even though the banks rely on individual private savings, they are so far from ordinary people that they no longer play a social role, as local banks once did.

Another increasingly multinational sector is natural resources, especially energy but also farm food products, minerals, chemicals and pharmaceuticals. The large multinationals guide consumer choices mainly through the tools of mass communications. Through persuasion techniques, such as psychological emulation, they influence large sections of the population. On the other hand, trade globalisation also exercises an influence through its distribution channels: enormous quantities of goods from all over the world are amassed in commercial centres, with repercussions on lifestyles and modes of consumption.

The consequence of this economic and financial aggregation beyond state borders is a kind of parallel power outside all controls, while the psychological and economic methods implemented tend to diminish individuals' critical judgement, as well as influence political choices, increasingly dependent on the big players in the global economy and finances.

Communities tend to be less rooted in local areas, which are no longer, as in preindustrial societies, the main source of subsistence. We have also lost the independent capacity to elaborate models of society, rich in individual and collective experience, that respond to the general condition of cultural diversity, when exchanges through trade and migrations were once a source of mutual enhancement. The deep changes in the last century can basically be summed up as the abandoning of rural areas and the concentration of millions of people in megalopolises and therefore the shift from a mainly agricultural and rural culture to a mainly urban and industrial culture.

We must now try and understand if what we have gained with the model of modern society and what we have lost with the end of the equilibrium between rural culture and industrial culture can be summed up in a new model, in which the values and achievements of both cultures coexist.

Textiles and fashion

Globalisation completed the process begun in the late 20th-century of the transition to a post-industrial or "meta-industrial" era, as some authoritative economists have called it. The new term stresses that we are talking about something that is no longer "after" but "beyond" the Fordist industrial model. Like the food sector, the textile and fashion sector still meets primary needs. But it was one of the first sectors to feel the effects of this transition period. Indeed in some countries the clothes industry has almost disappeared. Its companies have transferred their manufacturing activities to other areas of the world where low labour costs mean that production can still follow the classic industrial model. In Italy the phenomenon was less intense. There was a relatively smooth shift from the textile industry, characterised by classic manufacturing methods and measurable in the quantity of textiles produced, to the fashion industry, whose products are characterised by a high content of intangible elements, such as design, brand power, advertising with an emphasis on dream worlds and emulating celebrities. In short, all those kinds of components that are not simply functional. The current phase of transition will probably end with the dawning of a new era. For the moment it is difficult to envisage exactly what form it will take. But if we pan out to an all-round analysis of various aspects of the economy, sociology, ecology, anthropology and technology we may find a key to interpreting the ongoing phenomena: i.e. by reconsidering individual and social needs to grasp how to respond to the anxieties arising from contemporary society. The apparently constant demands in the new model include: the desire for a new relationship with the environment, a job with a decent living wage, access to intangible goods, such as culture in its widest sense (i.e. ranging from the cultural industry to intangible contents of products such as fashion and furniture goods), new forms of building, new town planning models, and even a new role for religious faith, which had been seen by the positivism underlying industrial societies as symbolising backwardness.

From the methodological point of view, it may be useful to compare the salient features of preindustrial society, simplistically written off as the legacy of an age characterised by poverty and ignorance. In fact once primary needs are satisfied, such as eating, health care, study and housing, intangible needs come to the fore. Arguably found more in preindustrial than in current society, intangible needs include pride in workmanship, creativeness, individual responsibility and forms of social caring. Moreover, they can also be extended to the importance of symbols in many aspects of life, including fashion, and of faith as a human response to the need for forms of transcendence as answers to questions which human reason cannot meaningfully provide.

If for our purposes here we simply consider a number of aspects in our relationships with nature and the organisation of the supply chain, what emerges is a need to respect equilibria. According to some experts, the failure to do so may lead to the disappearance – although not of the planet – at least of humankind. Globalisation is characterised by the geographical separation of production from consumption with its attendant exceptional rise in transport, international division of labour, and the excessive importance of the financial sector (and the growth of virtual finance that cyclically causes deep crises burning up individual savings). These features of globalisation also include the loss of skills in most manufacturing sectors. They have been replaced by production skills in intangible sectors, such as information technology, the so-called liberal professions, commerce and research, which employ, however, only limited sections of the population and in any case must be applied to the manufacturing industry. Since heavy industrialisation and the financial and environmental crises are evidence that globalisation cannot be the solution to the overall crisis in the Fordist model, what new model can we apply?

A possible solution may come from reconsidering the features of the new requirements in the supply chain: i.e. using local resources as much as possible, guaranteeing jobs and the survival of local skills, incorporating in products new distinctive elements of local culture and traditions as the intangible components valued by consumers, developing individual creativity and skills, and involving citizens in decision-making about their future. The result would be a society in which local aspects offset global aspects, which will inevitably continue to exist. What should emerge from an analysis of the critical points in the environmental system and in the economic world is a model in parallel to the current system based on concentrating production with high capital investments and wide-ranging internationalisation. This would not necessarily mean that a short supply chain is the alternative model but for the time being it may be complementary to the existing model. The short supply chain model could become important in terms of employment, and domestic production and consumption which have become urgent critical issues in the current globalised system. Changing this system requires research activity in all segments of the supply chain: from the production of the raw textile materials to spinning yarn and producing fabrics, tailoring techniques and, lastly, marketing. Marketing, in particular, requires a commitment in communications from public institutions when smaller businesses are not in a position to make the kind of investments required to make a big visible impact on the market.

This kind of system obviously requires a qualitative breakthrough from the cultural point of view so that the intangible quality of products and their content can be a distinctive feature and at the same time a way of raising customers' awareness, currently manipulated by commercial advertising without leaving any room for the critical capacity to choose.

In conclusion, if rethinking the industry is to be based on in-depth analysis then it will require investments in research and studies and greater debate on the issues. Since earliest antiquity, textile production and clothing have been one of the most important activities of human society. An heir to ancient civilisation, Italy developed excellent skills in this sector in the past. Indeed the crafts could even be used as a means to studying centuries of history. Today the sector is undergoing a deep crisis, mainly due to the relocation of manufacturing facilities in other parts of the world, where labour costs are lower. To tackle this theme comprehensively requires an analysis that begins with the structural elements of clothing in its various forms, from garments to footwear and other accessories. There are many elements involved in the development of the fashions that have characterised the various historical periods. An initial distinctive feature of textile production in past civilisations are the raw materials. In various areas in the world they were extracted from local resources, such as fibres from crops that had adapted to the local soil and climatic conditions. Thus cotton, for example, was produced in tropical areas, while linen and hemp were used in temperate areas. Fleeces were shorn from locally reared sheep in the Mediterranean and northern Europe, llamas and alpacas in the Andes and camels in North Africa. It was often not just a question of the specific features of a species but also of breeds selected in various world areas for the purpose.

Like the features of the material, the types of clothing were determined by function, whether to provide protection from the heat and sandy winds in tropical areas or from the cold in northern and mountainous zones. Always based on function, items of clothing have taken on various forms according to the activities of the people wearing them: military clothes were designed for the vigorous outdoor life; artisans wore their own specific working clothes, the blacksmith had a leather apron, while the chef had a cloth apron suited to kitchen work. But there are also hierarchical aspects (such as officers' uniforms and religious vestments) or status symbols.

This set of functions has intertwined with the development of local traditions leading to an infinite variety of clothing characterising different cultures: from the Scottish kilt to the Tyrolean *schützen*, the dress of Egyptian priests and clothes of the Indian castes. The functional aspect has thus combined with magic, religious, social, gender and also aesthetic aspects, defined by the play of colours and accessories, such as ornamental objects, necklaces, earrings, rings, various kinds of woven fibres, or by forms such as tunics or a dress modelled on the body.

This very rich heritage developed by various cultures was mostly lost after the industrial revolution, which only left economic and functional aspects and the consequent single model imposed by industrial civilisation. The industrial model certainly gave a very large number of people access to goods that previously had only been enjoyed in their best forms by a few social categories. At the same time, however, there was a loss of some values associated with the development of local cultures. Thus, for example, there was a loss in the sense of belonging often highlighted by clothing, which contributed to creating an identity and consequently giving meaning to daily life. This was before the onset of mass society, in which the strictly functional predominates. Since the human spirit tends to be irrepressible, some aspects sacrificed to standardised behaviour have re-emerged. This was the case, for example, with the success of the great tailors in the first half of the 20th century, the production of designer apparel in the second half of the 20th century or the models adopted by some rebellious groups, such as street wear.

These kinds of phenomena clearly challenge the rules of the global industry and market in which the only interest lies in increasing sales volume and consequently consumption. Now, on the eve of a cultural revolution like the Renaissance, to respond to the negative effects of industrial civilisation, the fashion industry must also begin to rethink its world by starting from an analysis of the meanings and values intrinsic to it.

Textile design and sustainability

To the background of considerations on a global scale, which range from environmental impacts to economic models, the development of cultures and values and a description of aesthetic canons, we set about tackling all aspects of the textile and clothing supply chain (from raw materials to tailoring techniques) in a joint project with the Tuscan Region, the Osservatorio dei Mestieri d'Arte dell'Ente Cassa di Risparmio di Firenze (a study centre for artistic crafts) and some Tuscan provinces. The first issue we addressed was that of achieving a more balanced use of natural resources and a reduction in transport. Today the textile fibre market uses around 50 percent natural fibres and around 50 percent man-made fibres.

In both cases the goods have to travel long distances with very negative repercussions in terms of greenhouse gases and pollution of the oceans and atmosphere. At the same time, sheep's wool, for example, once considered a resource to be exploited, is now simply treated as waste. In fact of the around 9,000 tonnes of wool produced in Italy, almost all is disposed as special waste. Although we are aware that there is a problem of wool quality driving consumption towards imported products, we believe that an in-depth analysis linked to research into technological innovations making at least part of Italian wool production more attractive could lead to a renewed use of this wool in various sectors, from clothing to furniture and industrial uses.

There is a similar picture as regards vegetable-origin fibres. These kind of fibres were once traditionally cultivated in Italy but they have now been abandoned: i.e. hemp and linen. Others, such as nettle and broom, were also cultivated although their use was more limited. Naturally we realise that it will be very difficult to reverse a trend that took almost a century to consolidate and is embedded in the industrial manufacturing world. We believe, however, that at a time of global crisis both in the environment and in the economy, a careful assessment of the potential use of local resources is opportune. Moreover, these resources not only include raw materials but also local expertise and knowledge. The use of industrial technologies rapidly made obsolete traditional skills that were still being used up to the Second World War throughout Italy. A culmination of centuries of civilisation, they are a unique heritage. The serious employment crisis in all industrialised countries is the consequence of a loss of skills and of an economic model that seeks labour wherever it costs less. We do not know if the trend is irreversible and neither do the economists, whose poor powers of prevision have been widely demonstrated by the current global crisis. So it is quite reasonable in terms of research to begin to look in the direction of local resources.

The supply chain in the project begins with the raw materials (wool or vegetable fibres, hemp, nettle and broom) and includes the various stages from preparation and spinning of the fibres, to weaving and the final tailoring to obtain personalised garments, which are high-quality from the point of view of the techniques adopted.

The project aims to highlight the critical issues in a supply chain characterised by the use of local natural resources and a series of artisanal stages. In fact although wool is available, the economic methods that emerged in the second post-war period have led to the disappearance of the skilled artisans required to transform the raw material into end products. For example, collecting and washing wool to remove impurities is carried out by specialised firms but today only very few survive. A single firm in Prato (Tuscany) washes lots of wool that are then sent to be processed for technological uses, such as heat insulation panels in the construction industry. These stages are followed by spinning and weaving. In this case too there are problems as regards the machines available today, since they are not suitable for fibres of lower quality in terms of length and thickness compared to imported wool.

This stage has involves a craft weaver working at Cutigliano in the Pistoia mountains and has led to the production of textiles in the natural colours of the Apennine breed of sheep, while another line has been developed in collaboration with a wool company, the Lanificio di Soci in Casentino (Arezzo), as far as finishing the textile is concerned, to obtain an ancient-type heavy woollen textile and a cloth which in the past was called the *panno carbiniere* because it was used for cloaks for *carabinieri* (a police corps); both of these textiles are fulled according to long-standing Italian traditions.

The last stage in the project has been entrusted to a tailoring company that produces made-to-measure male and female apparel mainly in fabrics from the Italian tradition using natural fibres and a choice of models based on traditional rural clothes, brought up to date for contemporary life and tastes.

The critical points in the supply chain are the time required to tailor made-to-measure clothes using high-quality techniques that require lengthy work with repercussions on the cost of production. An time-saving experiment was thus set up to use innovative tools in the various stages: computer assisted design (CAD) in preparing the patterns; tools to make cutting fabric easier; computerised systems for archiving patterns and online databases for the choice of fabrics.

In conclusion, the new era requires new formulas that can sum up the past and adopt the best aspects and achievements in line with human progress. To do this will require more thought, study and experimentation.

*CNR and the University of Florence

Select Bibliography

Madame Guerre, *Cours de Coupe*, Paris 1909 (Collection Familia).

M. & E. Theodore, *Les textiles. Histoire et travail*, Liège 1914 [1920].

J. Mathis, *Le livret du cordonnier*, Paris 1923.

J. B. Yernaux, *Le Cordonnier moderne*, Brussels 1933.

M. Beaulieu, *Le costume antique et médiéval*, Paris 1951.

D. du Puigaudeau, *Manuel pratique du tissage à la main*, Paris 1958.

G. Emlyn-Jones, *Make Your Own Gloves*, New York 1975.

M. Bona, F. A. Isnardi and S. L. Straneo (eds), *Manuale di tecnologia del tessile*, Bologna 1981.

C. McDowell, *Scarpe. Moda e fantasia*, Milan 1990.

Per filo e per segno. Viaggio nel mondo dell'arte tessile, Florence 1995.

J. Etienne-Nugue, *Mains de femmes*, Paris 1995.

E. Bolomier, *Le Chapeau. Grand art et savoir faire*, Paris 1996.

K. Wells, *Fabric Dyeing and Printing*, London 1997.

C. Cobb, G. S. Goodman and M. Wackernagel, *Why Bigger Is not Better: The Genuine Progress Indicator. 1999 Update*, San Francisco 1999.

F.-M. Grau, *Histoire du costume*, Paris 1999.

F.-M. Grau, *La haute couture*, Paris 2000.

G. Fereday, *Natural Dyes*, London 2003.

B. Galeskas, *Felted Knits*, Loveland 2003.

M. Schoeser, *Tessuti del mondo*, Milan 2003.

O. Bailloeul and F. Hamon, *Creations en feutre. Modeler la laine*, Paris 2004.

A. Donnanno, *Accessori moda. La tecnica dei modelli*, Milan 2004.

H. Worsley, *Un secolo di moda*, Cologne 2004.

F. Camilli and C. Screti, *Il panno blu*, Rome 2005.

G. Fouchard, *La mode*, Paris 2005.

M. P. Lebole, *Il sistema dell'artigianato artistico e tradizionale*, Fondazione per il Clima e la Sostenibilità, Florence 2005.

G. Maracchi, *L'arte di fabbricare gli zoccoli*, Florence 2005.

G. Maracchi, *Fabbricare pantofole e pianelle*, Florence 2005.

L. Bacci, S. Baronti and L. Angelini, *Manuale di coltivazione e prima lavorazione della ginestra per uso tessile*, Florence 2006.

G. Maracchi and F.P. Vaccari, "I cambiamenti del clima e la sostenibilità del pianeta", in *L'energia del nostro futuro. La seconda vita dell'agricoltura*, edited by R. Jodice and S. Masini, Rome 2006.

Natural. Tex. Le fibre naturali nella filiera tessile toscana, (Prato, Palazzo Novellucci, 17 November 2006).

E. Pagliarino and F. Cannata, "Il tessile fra tradizione e innovazione", in *Quaderni Orientamento e occupazione nei territori rurali*, 5, 2006.

Progetto Macro-Inn. Analisi macroeconomica del distretto tessile. I percorsi dell'innovazione, Florence 2006.

I. Schwegler and G. Maracchi, *Fabbricare cappelli*, Florence 2007.

Il tessile nel bacino del Mediterraneo, Bologna [2006?].

M. Ricchetti and E. Cietta (eds), *Il valore della moda. Industria e servizi in un settore guidato dall'innovazione*, Milan 2006.

L. Bacci, S. Baronti, N. Di Virgilio and S. Predieri, *Manuale di coltivazione e prima lavorazione dell'ortica per uso tessile*, Florence 2007.

L. Bacci, S. Baronti and L. Angelini, *Manuale di coltivazione e prima lavorazione della canapa da fibra*, Florence 2007.

L. Bacci, S. Baronti, L. Angelini and N. Di Virgilio, *Manuale di coltivazione e prima lavorazione del lino ed altre piante da fibra,* Florence 2007.

F. Camilli and A. Colombo, *Il merletto. La tradizione nelle mani*, Florence 2007.

Firenze. Guida ai mestieri d'arte, Florence 2007.

M. P. Lebole, B. Zini and G. Maracchi, *L'arte dell'intrecciare. Spiegata ai ragazzi*, Florence 2007.

L. Knight, *The Sewing Stitch and Textile Bible: An Illustrated Guide to Techniques and Materials*, Iola (Wisconsin) 2007.

Fabric. Textures & Patterns, Amsterdam 2008.

The Handbook of Style. A Man's Guide to Looking Good, New York 2009.

THE LABYRINTH OF LABELS AND CERTIFICATES

Lodovico Jucker

The search for more sustainable products and processes drives companies to commitments that go farther than what is required to meet current legislation and regulations. In many cases a company's commitment is supported by resorting to a certificate or label, especially to give credibility to requisites which by nature are often intangible insofar as they are features of processes that leave no traces on the end-product (e.g. the quality of labour used, the management of emissions in chemical fibre production, water consumption, etc).

"Certification is a written guarantee issued by a third party that the product or process conforms to specified requisites or that it has had a certain 'history' that cannot otherwise be communicated – or in extreme cases – believed."

A brand, or label, is a sign that the product in question conforms to the requisites stipulated in the certificate. In the world of textiles and clothing, concerns about sustainability have generated an intricated mass of logos and certificates and finding your way around it can be hard going. One reason for this proliferation is that we are talking about a very widespread new awareness that attracts the interest of new, often improvised operators, organisations, consultants and designers. A second reason is that in speaking about sustainability you might be referring to several different things: the safety of the product, social responsibility or strictly environmental themes. In fact the field still lacks a clear order and precise hierarchy.

A starting point: quality and environmental management systems

All schemes and kinds of branding presuppose companies intending to apply them have a basic grounding. Often implicit but at times expressly indicated as an initial condition, this consists in the company knowing its own products and processes and having an internal management system that checks objectives and the results of decision making. For this reason, the first stage on the road to sustainability is the adoption of a management model conforming to the two international standards ISO 9001 and ISO 14001.

So-called corporate management system "certification" imposes no regulations, however, as regards the ethical or environmental quality of products but basically serves two purposes: guaranteeing the market that an organisation is able to maintain what it promises in its contracts and offerings (ISO 9001 certification) and demonstrating to the market and to the public that it is aware of its own environmental impacts, which it attempts to manage in an appropriate way (ISO 14001).[1]

Issued by specialised qualified organisations, certification is now regulated by an international system in which the certifying bodies[2] are in turn inspected and monitored by accreditation agencies (in Italy ACCREDIA). ISO certification supplies the basic language for the first steps on the complex, multiform paths to sustainability.

First aspect: safe textiles

A sustainable product must first of all be safe. Although articles on the markets – at least in Italy – should be so anyway,[3] we can legitimately wonder why companies can conceivably make an even bigger commitment on this front and if the existing control system and regulations are not already sufficient to guarantee an adequate level of protection.

Historically this has not always been the case, at least until a few years ago, when the European Union decided to ban certain dyes accused of being cancerogenic. The safety of textile products is in fact primarily a question of chemicals in contact with the skin. Today this aspect, at least for those dyes considered to be dangerous, has been cleared up and governed by law and so there is only a risk when the laws are violated (possible when products are imported from not very reliable sources). Various studies are also focusing on the possible risks connected to other substances:

-formaldehyde, still used in finishing many fabrics;

-other dyeing agents, suspected of causing contact dermatitis;

-plasticisers or flame retardant products;

-pesticides or anti-mould products that in some way may enter the organism.

As regards these aspects, producers have an opportunity to make a commitment to improve their products before research results give rise to new legislative regulations and especially before measures of the European Community Regulation, REACH,[4] take full effect. Initially subject to considerable criticism, REACH is now fully operational. Its aim is to regulate the production and use of chemicals with the same severity as in the field of drugs and pharmaceuticals. According to the regulation, a substance can only be produced and used in textiles if it has passed initial scrutiny demonstrating it is harmless for consumers.

In the meantime, pending the completion of the tests on substances, manufacturers wishing to increase trust in its in own products can resort to other non-compulsory tools in the field that at times anticipate the work of REACH:

-The EU Ecolabel,[5] an environmental label created by the European Union according to specific criteria ensuring the absence of certain substances in end products.

-The Oeko-Tex 100 Standard.[6] This standard is owned by a private association of European laboratories which, despite the name, only certifies the absence of harmful chemicals in textiles.

-The SERI.CO certification[7] is associated with specifications introduced in the Como silk district; it includes a special card indicating harmful substances according to REACH criteria.

-L'Osservatorio sul Tessile Abbigliamento e Calzature ("Observatory on Clothing Textiles and Footwear), promoted by the Associazione Tessile e Salute ("Textile and Health Association),[8] is supported by companies, research institutes, medical organisations and business and consumer associations.

Set up in 2009 under the auspices of the Ministry of Health, the Observatory's task is to monitor the effects of products (textiles) on consumers' health (allergic reactions, dermatitis, etc). It has a database of harmful substances found in textile products[9] and is currently studying a project for the certification of companies who are willing to introduce product traceability in order to guarantee that there are no chemicals risks from their products.

The importance of chemical risks for consumers should not allow us to overlook the fact that textile product safety involves the management of two other kinds of risks: mechanical risk and textile flammability. Mechanical risk concerns the danger of suffocating, strangling, swallowing small parts and mainly concerns only some categories of consumers (children, sportspeople, the elderly, etc). Fire risk is currently regulated in Italy by law only for places open to the public or certain means of transport and for some categories of users. The field is completely unregulated for all clothing and furniture products used privately.

We must remember that for these aspects of textile product safety in Italy there is a technical report available to operators. Drafted by the Ente Nazionale Italiano di Unificazione (UNI), a national standards body, it provides a complete treatment of the subject, updated with the most recent findings.[10]

The UNI report also supplies analytical information on the state-of-the-art for individual aspects but also the specific limits on requisites needed to assess – when necessary – the degree of safety of a product.

Although social accountability can take many forms (from observing human rights to fiscal compliance, giving up corrupt practices, policies for local communities, the introduction of support initiatives, etc.), today in the supply chain producers interested in the sustainability of their products mainly have to deal with the aspects of working conditions in the various stages of the chain. The principles referred to and the related requisites are normally taken from the international declarations on human rights and the principles of the UN International Labour Organisation (ILO). In recent years the SA 8000 standard has been developed in this field. Created and managed by a private American association called Social Accountability, today it is the basis for the relevant certification, at times called "ethical".[11]

SA 8000 certification requires that companies adopt a management system guaranteeing the respect of principles such as no child or forced labour, non-discrimination, freedom of association, safety and health in the workplace and a decent living wage. As far as possible, the standard seeks to eliminate loopholes and therefore in the case of the supply chain requires that the same criteria are used by all suppliers upstream from the company certified, i.e. what in recent experience has been the most critical point in the system.

Certification is carried out by agencies accredited by the same American organisation and is based on audits in the field, at times without warning ("mystery audits"). Other initiatives focus on the quality of labour involved in the supply chain in low-wage countries:

-Fair Trade Initiatives[12] mainly committed to developing forms of fair trade in the field of food are also now active in the field of natural fibres.

-The Clean Clothes Campaign[13] is active in monitoring and denouncing unacceptable working conditions (it has no certification or trademark, however).

Everything gets much more complicated but also opens up new perspectives, when the path of sustainability crosses that of ecology. In recent years this relatively new discipline has been consolidating knowledge and methods to be used in assessing the "consumption of the environment" and defining the objectives for the conservation of the world's resources.

From the environmental point of view, all strategies for improvements, even with gradual and partial objectives, must begin from a global approach taking into account the life cycle of a product. The method of calculating the life cycle and its so-called environmental footprint is the Life Cycle Analysis (LCA), now well defined by a precise set of international technical regulations.[14] Constructed by taking into account the principal stages in the life of a product (raw materials, processing, distribution, use and disposal), the LCA calculates the main impacts that are generated (i.e. modifications to elements making up the environment: air, water, soil, natural resources, biodiversity, etc.).

But what do these analyses have to say about textile and clothing products? Although only a few studies have been conducted so far in this field and despite the very wide range of products, today some data are available. In the fairly well studied field of raw materials, the main critical issues concern (for natural fibres) the use of arable land (cotton), the consumption of water and energy (cotton), the consumption of non-renewable resources (man-made fibres), emissions into the atmosphere (man-made fibres), waste disposal in water and CO_2 emissions in general.

In processing, the critical areas are the consumption of energy, water and – in the finishing stages – the emissions of pollutants into the atmosphere (salts, surface-active agents, heavy metals, etc.). There are also significant impacts from the transport system, often intercontinental, and the associated considerable greenhouse gas emissions.

Recent research has identified the maintenance of textile products as a primary source of energy consumption, while the end of the life of products is still a mainly unexplored field. With a few exceptions, most garments still end up in rubbish dumps or are incinerated.

Taking action on each of these aspects means working towards a higher level of sustainability, although the goal of "zero impact" products is an ideal and not a realistic objective. The choice of aspect to be considered naturally depends on many technical type conditions, i.e. related to the possibility of finding real alternatives and the importance to be given to one environmental aspect rather than another at a given time. Green marketing is a subject now also being taught in Italy and is of great help in this kind of decision making.

Schemes and programmes from various kinds of environmental labels are useful in guiding decision-making, and especially in communicating a company's commitment to sustainability and the related results it has achieved.

Environmental labels

I will now consider some of the best-known environmental labels without making any claims to completeness, given the impossibility due to the tendency for many countries to create their own labels under local pressure. All these forms of certification are voluntary, although obtaining one may be an obligatory requisite for certain supplies (see, for example, the so-called "green purchases" of public administrations in Europe).

In general the procedure for obtaining a usage licence for a label is the same in all cases: a preliminary investigation, auditing of the organisation by a third party, testing campaign on products and subsequent monitoring activities. While some of these schemes enjoy official approval, others reflect private visions and interests. This can lead to less overall credibility and variations in emphasis depending which environmental aspects are held to be important.

1. Single-criterion labels

These labels are usually found on products mainly on the grounds of only one significant environmental feature which is described and guaranteed.
-The carbon footprint label[15] indicates the quantity of carbon emitted by a product during its life cycle, thus enabling consumers to compare products displaying this information. Although today the complex methods of calculating the carbon footprint are shared and defined by the British standard PAS 2050, there are still arbitrary criteria for extending or narrowing the boundaries of the life cycle being considered. This may give rise to fairly unreliable results and indications.
-A further variable of the carbon footprint is the indication of "carbon neutrality", if a producer has taken part in programme to offset its own emissions according to a controlled plan.
-The water footprint,[16] is similar to the carbon footprint but concerns the consumption of water resources.
-One special case concerns the use of recycled materials in fabrics, i.e. material removed from the waste cycle of discarded material, leftovers and also from post-consumer material (garments and other kinds of materials, such as PET packaging). In this case, too, the certification (which is a traceability label) guarantees the honesty of claims which otherwise would not be demonstrable.[17]

2. Organic textiles

In the wake of the success of organic food, in recent years, there has been a rise – starting in the United States – in the use of natural fibres produced according to organic farming regulations. These rules concern both criteria for land management (e.g. crop rotation and respect of biodiversity) and bans on chemical products and genetically modified crops. On the markets the biggest success story has featured the commonest natural fibre – cotton. Various kinds of certification schemes have been created to guarantee the integrity of the whole supply chain, bearing in mind that organic fibres and conventional fibres cannot be distinguished *a posteriori*. Today the most important are the Global Organic Textile Standard (GOTS)[18] and the Organic Exchange.[19] They have traceable schemes for raw materials but the GOTS also has criteria for the finishing processes and requisites of social responsibility.

3. Multi-criteria labels

The European Union's ECOLABEL guarantees consumers that a product respects environmental requisites in all the stages of its life cycle from the "cradle" to when it leaves the manufacturing facility. It thus includes the production of raw materials and their transformation into finished fabrics, from spinning to the article of clothing. The label establishes limits that cannot be exceeded in the production process as regards various aspects, such as the use of pesticides, water consumption and waste water, emissions into the atmosphere and the use of harmful substances. It also includes requisites about the safety of the product for the consumer. The ECOLABEL scheme, based on criteria established through public consultation, has become a model for other more or less regional, private or public labels that have had varying degrees of success in different countries:

-The BLUESIGN,[20] created in Switzerland, is based on five pillars (use of resources, consumer safety, atmospheric emissions, emissions into water, and health and safety in the workplace). It is a guarantee that manufacturers produce fabrics with a minimal polluting load, that their products are as harmless for the environment as possible and made with a minimal use of resources. The scheme monitors the whole production process and all the constituent parts of the product, so as to exclude the use of any harmful substances. The certification divides up the raw materials, compounds/substances and processes required to obtain the final product in three distinct categories (Blue, Grey and Black), which define the possibilities/limits for use: currently over 600 substances, either banned or whose use is limited, are monitored.

The United States CRADLE TO CRADLE certification[21] provides a method for quantifying the results of a production system designed to take into account the environment. This implies the use of healthy and safe materials from the environmental point of view, care over recycling, the use of renewable energy, search for efficiency in energy and water savings as well as strategies for social responsibility. Products that meet the requisites for this certification can be classed according to four categories (Basic, Silver, Gold and Platinum), which vary according to the requisites requested. There is also a toxicity rating (based on an assessment of hazards and routes of exposure for each substance and/or material used) divided into four categories (Green, Yellow, Grey and Red). Human health criteria are divided into two categories according to their harmfulness: Priority Criteria and Additional Criteria.

4. Towards a complete impact measurement

The vast variety of criteria that can be used and the range of aspects considered – not to mention the difficulty in measuring on a single scale the environmental profile of a product – have in recent years led to the creation of tools for analysing and managing data potentially offering reliable comparisons between products. As such they provide a support to correct environmental marketing. Firstly, some programmes were designed to construct indicators of products' environmental profiles rather than establishing thresholds or limits in the use of processes or substances. These indices are meant to accompany the products and supply information concerning various parameters relevant to each type of index:

-The American giant Walmart introduced a Sustainability Index in July 2009. It applies to all articles of mass consumption (including fabrics) and was conceived to provide information on aspects such as consumption of resources, greenhouse gases, waste and the quality of labour relations. All of these factors are used to guide consumers when choosing products. The initiative required a great deal of work in collaboration with universities and research centres to devise the indicators, standards, etc., and to make the information supplied through the index itself transparent and easy to understand.[22]

-In the same direction but through a legislative programme, the French government introduced the so-called "Grenelle Environment Agreement" (*Grenelle de l'environment*), approved in summer 2008. Within a complex strategy intended to steer activities and consumption towards more acceptable environmental standards, textile products will also be required to undergo severe scrutiny. The original text stated that "From 1 January 2011 the consumer must be informed by a label, brand, sticker or other appropriate means about the carbon footprint contents of products and their packaging as well as the consumption of natural resources and environmental impact of products during their life cycle."[23]

-The ECO-INDEX[24] is a recent environmental assessment tool introduced by the American and European outdoor industries (sport, trekking, camping, etc.) to help firms assess the environmental performance of their products at the design stage so they can choose their suppliers according to criteria that satisfy their environmental objectives. The index has been designed to apply to both semi-finished and finished products. It assesses the impacts in the six stages of the product life cycle: raw materials (including feedstock and processing), packaging, product manufacturing and assembly, transport & distribution, use and service, and end of life. It contemplates seven critical objectives (impact areas): land use intensity, water, waste, biodiversity, chemistry/toxics (people), chemistry\toxics (environment), and energy uses & greenhouse gases. The index has three different tools – guidelines, indicators and metrics – that may be used together or separately. The guidelines were conceived as an aid to planning. The environmental indicators with a comparative scoring system provide both qualitative and quantitative measurable parameters and include a tool for calculating the total score of product. The metrics of the environmental footprint are units of measure used to assess the environmental impact and calculate improvements.

5. The Environmental Product Declaration

The prototype or methodological benchmark for systems of environmental indicators was and still is the Environmental Product Declaration (EPD).

This certification system enjoys considerable authority for several reasons: it is based on a shared proven scientific method; it has already had considerable experience; and it is run by a Swedish public body in collaboration with the Ministry of the Environment, the academic world and the scientific community.

So far the system has tackled eighteen product categories.[25] It has established values for measuring impacts and created five classes summarising the measurements of all impacts. Only one category has been registered so far in the field of textile products: "orthogonal fabrics or knitwear made of synthetic fibres for sportswear, underwear and bathing costumes." An Italian company was one of the first to obtain this certification. The methodology begins by applying what is provided for in ISO regulations. It then provides a detailed reconstruction of resources, consumption and emissions of everything that is used and consumed (raw materials, ingredients, precursors, packaging, transport, etc.) in the product life cycle within a system that – for the meantime – goes from the cotton field (or oil well) to the shop shelf. Supplied in numerical form, the results make it possible to compare products in the same category and individual products' environmental performances.

Broad-spectrum labels

The multifaceted nature of sustainability has led to the creation of solutions that reflect more closely the complexity of the problems in the field and attempt to provide responses to several issues in a single label.

-The MADE IN GREEN[26] scheme – created and owned by Spanish trade associations – ensures that before buying a textile article consumers can check that the environment and workers' rights have been respected in all stages of the supply chain. A licence is granted for this label when the product is Oeko-Tex 100 certified, made by a company with ISO 1400, Oeko-Tex 1000, EMAS or the equivalent, and manufactured by organisations with social responsibility codes that include the AITEX standard, which in turn is based on SA 8000.

Environmental claims

Adopting a sustainability certification programme is a highly recommendable solution for most businesses, especially because to a greater or lesser extent the criteria for certification are not subjective but come from wider outside consultation.

At the same time many companies prefer a more direct contact with the public and therefore without the mediation of certifying bodies. This leads to a large number of self-declared environmental claims made by producers about the intangible and putative environmental and/or social properties of their products.

The self-declared method inevitably lends itself to abuses of public credulity, even at times in good faith. That is why anyone using this tool today is subject to rules and recommendations aimed at curbing any possible vagueness and grey areas.

The standard reference on the subject is ISO 14021, which contains the requisites for a green claim that is honest, legal, decent and truthful. According to this standard,

self-declared environmental claims and all explanatory statements:

a) shall be accurate and not misleading;

b) shall be substantiated and verified;

c) shall be relevant to that particular product, and used only in an appropriate context or setting;

d) shall be presented in a manner that clearly indicates whether the claim applies to the complete product, or only to a product component or packaging, or to an element of a service;

e) shall be specific as to the environmental aspect or environmental improvement which is claimed;

f) shall not be restated using different terminology to imply multiple benefits for a single environmental change;

g) shall be unlikely to result in misinterpretation;

h) shall be true not only in relation to the final product but also shall take into consideration all relevant aspects of the product life cycle in order to identify the potential for one impact to be increased in the process of decreasing another;

i) shall be presented in a manner which does not imply that the product is endorsed or certified by an independent third-party organization when it is not;

j) shall not, either directly or by implication, suggest an environmental improvement which does not exist, nor shall it exaggerate the environmental aspect of the product to which the claim relates;

k) shall not be made if, despite the claim being literally true, it is likely to be misinterpreted by purchasers or is misleading through the omission of relevant facts;

I) shall only relate to an environmental aspect that either exists or is likely to be realized, during the life of the product;

m) shall be presented in a manner that clearly indicates that the environmental claim and explanatory statement should be read together. The explanatory statement shall be of reasonable size and in reasonable proximity to the environmental claim it accompanies;

n) shall, if a comparative assertion of environmental superiority or improvement is made, be specific and make clear the basis for the comparison. In particular, the environmental claim shall be relevant in terms of how recently any improvement was made;

o) shall, if based on a pre-existing but previously undisclosed aspect, be presented in a manner that does not lead purchasers, potential purchasers and users of the product to believe that the claim is based on a recent product or process modification;

p) shall not be made where they are based on the absence of ingredients or features which have never been associated with the product category;

q) shall be reassessed and updated as necessary to reflect changes in technology, competitive products or other circumstances that could alter the accuracy of the claim;

r) shall be relevant to the area where the corresponding environmental impact occurs.

The same concepts were recently taken up again by the International Chamber of Commerce (ICC) which in January 2010 published a proposal to supplement and modify its own ICC Code of Advertising and Marketing Communication Practice (2006).

Today many believe this code to be the most authoritative standard for the world of advertising and the institutions and bodies regulating trade and business. The change aims to make an updated and stricter overall framework for "responsible environmental communications to the market".[27]

While the ICC code previously considered as unacceptable any sustainability claim for a product, "since there are no generally accepted methods for measuring sustainability and to corroborate the results achieved". The subsequent proliferation of green claims and the growing interest in environmental sustainability has led to such claims being accepted but according to precise conditions: i.e. the companies must have the requisites to be credible. The new code aims to stop greenwashing practices by companies who overstate the environmental benefits of their products, thus reducing consumer trust and penalising those who do not make misleading claims.

The new code offers a guide for tackling environment claims and the criteria for comparing and assessing them. In fact they are the same as the ISO specifications listed above.

A roadmap for businesses

In this complex detailed situation in danger of being outdated daily by the creation of new initiatives, businesses have difficulty in finding a reliable roadmap, given that no scheme or certificates can guarantee *a priori* the commercial success of a green marketing project. It is up to the fashion companies, as a function of the specific objectives they assign to a product or collection, to identify a type of label or certification on which to base the plausibility of their projects.

Table 1 provides an overview as an aid in choosing the relevant label. It seeks to summarise the indications that we have provided, classifying various schemes according to the "aspects" or "phases" they are meant to regulate. It must be pointed out, however, that the schemes have different assessment methods:

some require fixed requisites or values/thresholds as limits not to be exceeded; some have a scoring system; and some involve the construction of overall indices for benchmarking purposes.

Notes
[1] Similar to the ISO 14001, the European Union EMAS scheme is only applicable in Europe.
[2] CERTITEX is a specialised Italian agency dedicated only to the textile, clothing and footwear sectors (www.certitex.com.)
[3] See the Italian "Consumer Code" that implemented the EU Directives on manufactures' responsibility and the overall safety of products.
[4] EC Regulation no. 1907/2006.
[5] www.eco-label.com.
[6] www.oeko-tex.com.
[7] www.seri.co.it.
[8] www.tessileesalute.it.
[9] The various awareness-raising initiatives include the consumer leaflet entitled *Ma sai cosa ti metti addosso?* ("Do you know what you are wearing?") promoted by the Associazione Tessile e Salute in collaboration with the Piedmont Region Trade Department; the leaflet was distributed in clothes shops and shopping centres.
[10]. See the technical report UNI TR 11359:2010 available on www.uni.com. UNI is the Italian organisation responsible for drafting voluntary technical regulations for all sectors; UNI represents Italy in the European Committee for Standardization (ECS) and the International Standard Organisation (ISO).

Table 1.

Label / scheme	product safety	social responsibility	environment				
			wastewater	CO_2 consumption	water consumption	atmospheric emissions	only organic fibres
ECOLABEL	*		*			*	
OEKOTEX 100	*						
SERI.CO	*	*					
ORGANIC EXCHANGE							*
SA 8000		*					
FAIR TRADE		*					
MADE IN GREEN	*	*	*			*	
GOTS			*				*
CRADLE TO CRADLE			*	*	*	*	
BLUE SIGN	*	*	*		*	*	
ECO index			*	*	*	*	*
SCS							
EPD			*	*	*	*	

[11] For Italy, see www.lavoroetico.org.

[12] www.fairtrade.org.

[13] www.cleanclothes.org.

[14] See the ISO 14040 regulations (www.iso.org).

[15] www.carbonfootprint.com.

[16] www.quantis-intl.com/waterfootprint.php.

[17] The most popular certification standard today – albeit still only with a limited circle of users in the United States – is the Scientific Certification Systems (SCS); www.scscertified.com.

[18] www.global-standard.org.

[19] www.organicexchange.org.

[20] www.bluesign.com.

[21] www.cradletocradlehome.com.

[22] www.walmartfacts.com.

[23] See the modification to Article 85 of the *Code de consommation* and Law no. 2009-967, 3 August 2009, on the programme to implement the *Grenelle de l'environnement*.

[24] www.ecoindexbeta.org.

[25] www.environdec.com.

[26] www.madeingreen.com.

[27] ICC Document No. 240-46/557, 14 January 2010 [www.iccbo.org/]. In addition to general principles, it includes a check list for assessing environmental claims. On the same subject see also the *Green Claims Code* (2000) issued by the UK Ministry of the Environment, Transport and Regions (www.dft.gov.uk/e), the *Guide for the Use of Environmental Marketing Claims* by the US Federal Trade Commission and the UK government guide *Making a Good Green Claim* (www.defra.gov.uk/corporate/consult/green-claims/index.htm).

end of life	recycled material	notes
		only for cotton products
		only for natural fibres
*	*	
*	*	
	*	
*		

TEN KEY STEPS TOWARDS SUSTAINABLE FASHION

Fabio Guenza

Introduction

By definition fashion lives on permanent innovation. Not everything that is innovative is also sustainable but today sustainability is one of the principal if not *the* principal driver of innovation and change in the industry, as well as being a crucial field for research and experimentation. One of the main features of sustainable innovation is that its introduction implies sweeping systemic changes. It does not only mean using green technologies or simply drafting a social report (or a corporate social responsibility report) alongside the financial statement or passively adapting to new environmental and social laws. Sustainability is the result of integrating many elements: strategies, products and processes, organisation, management systems, corporate culture, communications and reporting. Sustainable innovation mobilises resources that go beyond strictly corporate resources. There can be no sustainability if company administrators fail to take on the tasks of responsibly managing the effects that the corporate decisions have on the wider world of stakeholders – from workers and consumers to local communities in all fields (economic, environmental, social and ethical). Similarly, there can be no sustainability if the stakeholders do not do likewise, supporting and encouraging the business in this drive and solving its internal conflicts of interest.

The second distinctive aspect of fashion is the prevalence of the intangible over the material nature of products. By their very nature aesthetic and stylistic factors are subjective and dominate the more objective, functional factors. This means that, on one hand, the intrinsically material and social values informing sustainability become more peripheral (efficiency in using resources, savings, care over the measurable impact on the environment and society) while, on the other, there is a growing need to adapt production processes to the changes that take place in the cultural sphere and exercise an influence over consumption. These two factors – permanent innovation, which translates into permanent change, and the key role of the intangible – set the goalposts for the challenge of sustainability. To move on this ground requires pragmatism, experience and specific knowledge. All of these are needed on the path to sustainability that must be organised in a series of practical steps. The list of these steps is inevitably sequential but the same cannot be said of the path: some steps may be taken in parallel and not in series and there can be many interactions between one step and another.

We can outline four main stages on the path to sustainability: exploration (Steps 1,2,3), designing (Steps 4,5,6,7), implementation (Steps 8,9) and full operation (Step 10).

Exploration

Step 1: how much of what companies already do is sustainable?
The first step, the step we begin from is… understanding that we are actually some way down the path and that the company already has a more or less big impact on the economic, social and environmental system. It is a question of assessing (or self-assessing) the forms already used by the company and its management to tackle the issue of sustainability. We can identify some typical approaches that companies adopt:

-*Rejection or paternalism*. Although not the same thing, they often go together. Possible well-meaning efforts in favour of sustainability are due to personal sensitivity and not from a real process of taking on board the expectations and aspirations of all those stakeholders who have an interest in, or are influenced by a company's actions. These efforts are not configured as elements built into company life but as residual and ancillary forms of generosity.
Possible beneficial initiatives are not connected to the core business and therefore reflect philanthropy rather than corporate citizenship. This is a particularly common approach on the Italian market;

-*Custom-made*. This is a reactive approach. The company reacts to outside pressure to assume responsibility. It is typical of a company subject to a negative campaign, for example, calling into question the ethics of its supply chain (unfair working conditions, child labour, etc.). The company reacts by developing a responsible management system. In other countries it has often been the starting point for stakeholder engagement policies on a large scale. The best-known examples are the big sportswear brands which in the last decade were the target of large-scale campaigns by consumer organisations, activists and humanitarian organisations;

TEN KEY STEPS TOWARDS SUSTAINABLE FASHION

-*Compliant.* This may be a reactive or proactive approach. In both cases it involves adopting common standards and codes of conduct without particularly taking into account the interests expressed by the company's specific stakeholders. The approach can be defined as reactive if the choice is in some way imposed by customers or suppliers and necessary to keep up with the market; it is, on the other hand, proactive when the choice is the outcome of the company's independent will to show its own degree of adhesion to the principles of sustainability;

-*Tactical, partial, short-term.* This is the case when a company sees some aspects of sustainability as opportunities to be managed and equips itself to harvest the best objective results independently of any general approach to sustainability. This is typically found in short-term tactical green marketing actions, which do not address the problem of possible attendant future expectations;

-*Strategic and integrated.* This approach is found when the company reckons that each aspect of sustainability is a variable to be managed in an integrated systematic way and makes arrangements to do so at various levels of the organisation. At the centre of this approach is broadened governance in which the responsibility for management also takes into account the interests of all stakeholders.

Step 2: planning an integrated path

Whatever the result of the first step, to make progress on the path requires a solid, consistent and logical approach. The elements of social responsibility must be built into the company's governance, strategies and policies. There are specific tools for doing this, such as stakeholder engagement, or specific techniques, such as the social and environmental impact management systems. But firstly normal management tools must be used. The path to sustainability is arguably the most classical example of a continuous improvement process to which a managerial technique can be applied, such as the so-called Deming Cycle – after Edwards Deming who devised it (Deming 1968) – or PDCA (Plan-Do-Check-Act). It is not enough simply to do and do and do, you must "plan, do, check and act."

-*Planning.* This means defining a sustainability plan with policies, objectives, activities and indicators in order to measure results in terms of ethical, social and environmental performances;

-*Doing.* Implementing planned activities. Adopting a modular approach is usually advisable with the application of the plan in initially circumscribed situations; for example, the field of the application for an environmental management system for health or security may initially be limited to a single production department, or one company in a group, and/or a specific level of subcontracting. This field can then be gradually extended, once the result of the application has been checked and adapted with suitable improvements;

-*Checking*. Checking the match between the activities carried out and those planned and the results obtained with those expected; introducing suitable adjustments to policies, objectives, activities and indicators initially devised in the planning stage;

-*Acting*. Readjusting the activities to maintain or improve the process. Firstly, the organisational aspects must be adjusted: this involves identifying the people, means and modes for managing the path. In other words, integrating sustainability governance into corporate governance with an initial attribution of responsibility, roles and delegated tasks, starting from the top. At this stage companies can begin to involve a possible dedicated resource, either internal or outsourced (CSR manager, sustainability officer, facilitator, etc).

Step 3: auditing sustainability

Starting from the results of self-assessment (Step 1), which measures the degree of awareness and kind of corporate culture, a more detailed, in-depth analysis is required. This is not necessarily to establish a complete or definitive picture, but to outline a more overall design that will subsequently be modified and enhanced over time. Step 3 thus involves describing the identity of the company, not at as it is imagined, but how it is in reality, by means of two kinds of analyses:

-*Internal survey*: what parts of company life are involved in sustainability? What values and actions expressing a responsiveness to sustainability issues have been built into corporate behaviour? What initiatives have been introduced for the economic management of environmental impacts? Does the company take into account non-economic interests of external stakeholders? What is the management's attitude towards CSR issues? What is the overall corporate culture on the issue of sustainability?

-*Benchmarking*. Applying a similar analysis to rivals can establish mutual positioning in terms of sustainability.

After this survey the vast majority of companies will probably discover that they have already voluntarily – and more or less purposefully or programmatically – started up initiatives on environmental, social or ethical issues directly connected to their businesses (without considering therefore acts of generosity). This might involve actions such as devising a low environmental impact product, improving workers well-being, etc.

The work of surveying and initial analysis can be carried out independently or with the help of outside consultants (facilitators, CSR and sustainability analysts).

Designing

Step 4: redefining identity; vision, mission and values

Comparing the results in Step 3 with the sustainable identity that the company aims to achieve will probably produce a more or less pronounced gap. Step 4 is indispensable in closing that gap, making appearance and substance, and image and reality meet. Closing the gap will involve a change of perspective, a strategic shift that must be considered as a long-term decision. To implement it, in fact, the company begins by redefining its mission, vision and basic values. The changes may be radical and imply very long timelines:

-*Vision* of the future, possible risks and opportunities. This involves responding to questions concerning industrial, cultural, social and environmental trends. For example, how will regulations on environment, safety, labour relations and social standards evolve and influence the company's business? Can anticipating as a deliberate choice what will later be required by law give a company a competitive advantage and a better reputation with consumers? What pressures will come from climate change and scarce resources? What will be the influence of CO_2 emissions in the atmosphere generated by transport on a global scale in the supply chains and the great distance between production areas and consumption areas? How will consumers' attitudes and preferences change? Especially in relations to sustainability? What will be the effect on markets of the arrival of new brands modelled from the outset to be sustainable? What kind of challenge will they bring? Are there are any ideas to be grasped and re-proposed?

-*Mission*. This is the main distinctive element separating one business from another. All companies aim to supply value to their owners or shareholders. Fashion companies produce and sell products and supply accessory services. But not all have the same past and the same philosophy, the same individual way of interpreting their own role on the markets in supplying their products or services. The mission is the response of the company as an organism to the eternal question of the individual: Who am I? Where do I come from? Where am I going? Why do I exist? Only the company itself can answer these questions. What are the company's roots? What was the founding spirit? What direction has it taken? What is its corporate philosophy?

-*Values*. There are various ways of achieving an aim. Decisions and actions that will be made by individuals belonging to the company will depend on corporate values. Reflecting the company culture and tradition, the values guide company behaviour and all those working in it or on its behalf. Ethical values define duties and responsibilities in the relationships between companies and their stakeholders (see Step 5). Sustainability requires the affirmation of certain values, either new or revived. These values must be clearly identified and explicitly affirmed and must inspire the company's decisions and actions.

Step 5: the ethical code

Companies work in situations that are always breaking down and recomposing. Society changes, the market changes, companies change and fashion companies in particular constantly change.

What is required, then, is an action guide, a set of rules or code to inform the behaviour of the company and the people who work in it. Here we must clear up one aspect already mentioned in the previous pages. The path towards sustainable and responsible behaviour leads to the continuous search to reconcile the interests, aspirations and expectations of all stakeholders associated with or influenced by the company's actions. Dividends for shareholders, wages, jobs, safeguarding local communities, subcontractors' interests, product quality and reasonable prices for customers are all elements that concur to define conciliation.

Sustainability tends to encourage the convergence of interests and expectations but these may be and often are conflicting. If one or several stakeholders feels their own interests and expectations are not satisfied by the company (low dividends, low salaries or job losses, for example, because of relocation policies, negative impacts on the environment and local society, unsatisfactory or overly expensive products), they may decide to make their own voice heard (protests, strikes, local government sanctions, consumer complaints) or even to leave the company and move to – or work for the benefit of – rivals who offer better, more satisfactory solutions.

Corporate management has every interest to attract and maintain stakeholders in the business. The problem is that the continuously changing scenario and the need to make decisions can often generate tensions between stakeholders that may degenerate into outright conflict, if not suitably managed. The only practical feasible solution is to establish a relationship of trust. Trust is a fundamental value that can bind stakeholders and company business. The logic of social responsibility is based on respect for freely assumed commitments over time and this mechanism generates trust. More in general, trust is a shared asset of key importance for market operations and improves the trusted company's competitive positioning. Moreover, trust requires solid anchoring. A key way of anchoring trust is to subscribe to an ethical code as a pact agreed around the company's business aims, inspiring principles and the rules governing it – from the highest level down to details dictated by management needs and circumstances.

The code is an ethical infrastructure governing the behaviour of people working in a company and towards the outside world in pursuing its objectives. Implementing the code involves introducing organisational support structures, such as ethical officers, ethical committees and internal ethical auditing. Their task is to check that processes and behaviour comply to the stated principles and to gather and respond to reports, queries, etc.

The best way to ensure that the management of the organisation reflects the ethical vision of the company and provides adequate, transparent guarantees is to draw up a formal set of rules for behaviour in the decision-making processes and business activities: i.e. an ethical code. The code may also include premises for the rules of behaviour. For example, it is useful to formalise in clear statements the company's mission, which from this point of view concerns not only the ownership and management but also all the other stakeholders, including employees, customers and suppliers, consumers and local communities. It would be very difficult, for example, to establish dialogue with stakeholders' representatives or clear up a company's own positions as regards possible media criticism or campaigns, if not by beginning from a clear, public mission statement. The same line of reasoning can be applied to vision, values, the criterion for tradeoffs, up to the rules of behaviour. All of these elements may justifiably be said to require single documents but, since they are all interconnected and will remain so, they can equally justifiably be included in an ethical code.

ORGANISATIONAL MODEL as per Legislative Decree 231/2001 of the Italian Government

---

The planning of the ethical code may often be integrated into the design of the organisational model. There are obviously affinities that can make such a decision timely and economical, although normally this is thought to apply to large companies..

It is worth making a digression on smaller-sized firms. In fact there are good reasons why this kind of model should be adopted by companies of any size, although of course with investment of resources proportional to the size of the company. "Because of the nature of its business activities, is the company exposed to risks concerning safety in the workplace that may involve serious or very serious damage to employees, collaborators and subcontracting companies that work in the company's production areas? Is the company in charge of its workers outside the company's production areas? If the answer is yes, even to only one of these two questions, then the company is strongly recommended to apply [Decree] 231" (source: "Check-list sul DLgs 231/2001, Sindaci & Revisori", Il sole 24 ore, February 2008).

Although a voluntary tool, the model pursuant to LD 231 is contemplated by the law and has far from negligible consequences from the legal point of view.
Re: an organisational shortcoming in the company involves criminal responsibility for a crime committed by an individual employed in the company. To whom it applies: any organisation presumed responsible for crimes committed in its interest or to the advantage of people in senior management positions, unless it has an adequate organisational model (shifting of the burden of proof). Various crimes can be charged starting from crimes against the public administration; particularly pertinent in this case are those concerning the environment and safety in the workplace. Paradoxically, shifting of the burden of proof, with its commitment of resources and time and risks involved and the size of the sanctions, which are large even simply for neglectful behaviour albeit with a powerful social and environmental impact means that companies are very strongly

recommended to adopt this tool, especially smaller-sized companies, which are less well-prepared than large ones to absorb events of a certain absolute importance. The sanctions, for example, may be translated into: a. confiscation of the profits (always); b. (if responsibility is proven) economic penalties (e.g. even from 285,000 to 1,500,00 euros for fatal accidents) and disqualification for a year or more (as regards authorisations, licenses, permits, contracts with the public administration, grants, financings, contributions or subsidies, even those already allocated, which must then be returned). The guidelines were conceived for large companies and are inadequate for small- and medium-size firms. This lacuna must be filled as soon as possible.

Step 6: Mapping relations and interests. The stakeholders

As we have seen, the adoption of sustainable behaviour translates into improved relations with stakeholders. The sixth step involves mapping a clear, detailed view of the company stakeholders, their interests and expectations, who effectively represents them, and what forms can be used to establish a dialogue. Moreover, the more important stakeholders must be identified, i.e. those with greater influence on the results of business (those who can create a crisis for the company, delay the realisation of objectives, etc). Step 6 is thus implemented through a mixed set of actions:

-*Identifying stakeholders*. This practical work, bound to the specific activities of the company, involves making a detailed description of stakeholders' profiles: who represents and interprets their interests, which unions, opinion leaders and consumers' organisation…? Can various segments with different interests be identified, for example, classing consumers according to age, income, lifestyle etc.? What is their geographical location (local players, national, from other countries or international, like NGOs or UN agencies)? What is their economic influence (small, large, very large)?

-*Identifying expectations*. What expectations do stakeholders have of the company and how often? What is their possible contribution to corporate strategies, for example, the role that consumers are taking on for companies as co-designers or co-producers?

-*Ranking*. How far can stakeholders influence the company's activities? Mapping out stakeholders requires an analysis starting from inside the company, by creating workgroups, interviewing managers, collecting information etc. At the same time there must also be effective monitoring of outside interlocutors. A company normally forms its own idea of what its interlocutors think and expect, but it is indispensable to check them out directly with tools like focus groups, interviews with opinion leaders, public opinion surveys and market research. Lastly, the results of the mapping must be clear and visible for all managers in a formal way and therefore must be explicitly translated into detailed reports. An example of a not necessarily exhaustive list of stakeholders to take into consideration may include those who are directly involved in economic relations with the company and all those who can influence the company's action or be influenced by them.

Among those directly involved are, for example:

-*Employees*. Companies are the people who work in them. Attracting and holding onto the best talents, loyalty and job motivation do not depend only on economic factors but also on involvement, a good working environment and the career opportunities that the company offers;

-*Financiers*. Firstly the owners and then the shareholders, if it is a joint stock company, but also those (citizens, workers and consumers) who, following the 2003 reform of Italian company law, can participate in the life and capital of the company through financial tools other than shares and bonds. They thus now have the right, for example, to vote on specifically indicated subjects, such as appointing an independent member of the board of directors or the supervisory committee or an auditor. There are also financial institutions. Stock-exchange investors' interest in sustainable companies is evidenced by the existence of dedicated stock-exchange indices (such as the FTSE4GOOD or the Dow Jones Sustainability Index) and by rating agencies specialised in CSR and non-financial analysis of companies' sustainability;

-*Consumers*. They search for reasonably priced products and in any case in line with the features of the product, but also quality, identity, security and environmental and ethical content;

-*Customers and suppliers*. Each company needs carefully fostered relationships and mutual advantages with its own partners. Whether they are looking for franchisees or customers they must be able to convince their own business partners that they are the company who will guarantee greatest added value. In addition to economic aspects, trust can be a crucial factor.

Among stakeholders not directly involved in business relations we find, for example:

-*Communities and organisations in civil society (NGOs, associations, etc)*. A company's capacity to build a good reputation to an increasing extent depends on relationships with local communities and consumer and environmentalist organisations, active citizens and non-profit organisations. Especially during downturns when fewer funds are available for donations, maintaining good relations with stakeholders and channelling resources into projects for good causes as pertinent as possible to the core business may help improve the company's image and prevent conflicts that could be disastrous during crises;

-*Local communities and institutions* (local and national government, research centres, universities, national ombudsmen and international authorities) may influence business through restraints (laws, regulations and sanctions) and opportunities (various forms of support, funding, the generation of positive external effects, etc).

Step 7: sustainability planning

Defining the objectives of sustainability and the strategies to realise them is the result of analysing the corporate identity (Step 4), the relevant stakeholders expectations (Step 6) the distance between the starting point and the pre-established target (Step 3) and the amount of available resources.

Planning of actions is carried out by considering:
-the type of CSR approach the company has (cf. Step 1);
-previous experience (cf. Step 3);
-likely scenarios: the evolution of regulations, market, competition, society, etc. (cf. Introduction and Step 4);
-corporate identity (cf. Step 4 and 5);
-stakeholder expectations (cf. Step 6);
-the analysis of the critical points in the organisation: products and processes, management systems, communications and reporting systems, corporate culture;
-analysis of critical points and possible improvements to the company's supply chain;
-the assessment of innovative solutions for critical issues;
-the analysis of successful solutions adopted by rivals and in other sectors;
-the assessment of available resources.

A proper sustainability plan identifies:
-macro objectives and strategies for achieving them;
-objectives and choices of behaviour that the company aims to adopt, also in terms of CSR tools, including the drafting of stakeholder engagement policies;
-key resources, the assignment of responsibilities in determining suitable schedules;
-operational and methodological tools for improvements;
-a system of process indicators and results chosen for measurement;
-periodical revision of the plan itself.

In operational terms, this means:
-designing policies and objectives for each aspect of corporate management;
-building consensus within the company on the need for change and improvement;
-identifying strengths, weaknesses, opportunities and threats to business with reference to stakeholder expectations;
-checking consistency between policies and objectives, assessing risks and opportunities;
-checking the human resources and materials required to develop the plan;
-identifying processes and resources involved in the strategies;
-identifying the departments responsible and possibly when necessary adding new roles;

-drafting a joint action plan (with schedules, responsibilities, activities, etc);
-designing the solutions and checking their validity, initially on a small scale;
-drafting working procedures and regulations for sustainability reporting.

Implementation

Step 8: developing social responsibility measures

Step 8 is the actual implementation of the planning drafted in Step 7. "Doing" is not the only activity, however. Periodically monitoring the state of progress of the activities and the results obtained as well as assessing actions are equally important. Have the objectives been reached?

Do practices, behaviour and working procedures effectively comply to the established code? In which fields has their been defaulting? How can it be avoided in future?

In operational terms, indicators must be established for:
-monitoring the efficiency of the sustainability projects (reaching objectives);
-monitoring the efficiency of intangible structures (culture and organisation) and tangible structures (technology, finances, etc.) to guarantee the operational and management conditions required to achieve the sustainability objectives;
-implement revision and integration processes in company practice, including the suitability of the ethical management system (code and indicators).

Step 9: assessing and reporting results

Each company assesses and reports on its economic and financial results – for example, through financial statements, auditing reports, analysis of financial flows, etc. – not only to shareholders, but also to third parties, such as the tax authorities, banks, etc. Making progress on the path of sustainability requires similar care over assessing and reporting environmental and social aspects.

Social and environmental accounting tools must thus be adopted. They require the systematic collection of qualitative and quantitative data and the calculation of social and environmental indicators as yardsticks of sustainability.

Corporate practice has approached in various ways the set of documents required to assess and report on the sustainability performance of companies: environmental reports, social accounting, CSR reports and sustainability statements.

The sustainability report, however, combines all these aspects in a single public document which assesses the value created by the so-called triple bottom line, which takes into account not only profit but all three Ps of sustainability: profit, people and planet.

This is not the place to go into the vast literature on methods for drafting sustainability reports, nor to list existing good practices.

But it is worthwhile stressing that these documents should also include third-party assessments, not so much for the purposes of certification, as happens with financial statements but for the sake of including the assessment that stakeholders make of corporate sustainable performances. This is often done by adding interviews to documents or by monitoring stakeholder satisfaction.

The following excerpt is a quote from an Italian Order of Accountants document on how to report on social and environmental aspects within the annual report, as contemplated by Article 2428 of Italian Civil Law.

```
| ---------------------------------------------------------------
| COMPULSORY NON-FINANCIAL REPORTING
| ---------------------------------------------------------------
| "The CNDCEC (Consiglio Nazionale dei Dottori Commercialisti e Esperti Contabili [Na-
| tional Council of Accountants and Bookkeepers]) believes... that recourse should be
| made to non-financial indicators only when they are really necessary to understand the
| situation of a company and the results of the financial year. But, since the legislator has
| specified 'information relevant to the environment and the personnel', the CNDCEC
| believes that this specific information must be seen with a view to reinforcing the social
| role of the company and, thus, obligatorily – and therefore, independently of the impor-
| tance of the related economic effects on the annual report – information in Annex III
| must be included in the annual report, if correlated events have taken place (CNDCEC,
| "La relazione sulla gestione – art. 2428 codice civile").
|
| ---------------------------------------------------------------
| Annex III Information on the environment and personnel
| ---------------------------------------------------------------
| Compulsory information on personnel:
| -death in the workplace of personnel in the employee register, for which a definitive
| corporate responsibility has been ascertained;
| -major accidents in the workplace that have involved serious or very serious injury to
| personnel in the employee register for which a definitive corporate responsibility has
| been ascertained;
| -accusations concerning workplace illness by employees and former employees due to
| mobbing, for which the company has been definitively declared responsible, describing
| the nature and the extent of such charges.
| Compulsory information on the environment:
| -damage to the environment for which the company has definitively been declared
| guilty;
| -definitive sanctions or penalties imposed on the company for environmental crimes or
| damage;
| -greenhouse gas emissions as per Law 316/2004 (obligatory for factories subject to the
| Emissions Trading Scheme (ETS) and optional for all other companies).
| Optional information on the environment and personnel:
| -initiatives to convert previously temporary work contracts into permanent contracts;
| -investments in personnel (security) and related operating costs;
| -environmental investments and environmental costs (according to Recommendation
```

| 2001/453/EC, i.e. investments and environmental costs that improve environmental im-
| pacts but distinguish them from those required to meet the criteria established by law);
| -waste disposal or recycling policies, if important;
| -certificates (SA 8000; EMAS; ISO 14000; DM SAS); – greenhouse gas emissions as per
| Law 316/2004 and any green certificates, if the company does not operate in a sector for
| which such information is obligatory.

Step 10: full operation

The tenth step is completed when the sustainability plan for the company is integrated into the industrial plan and the human resources are operational at all levels.

But this step is never really completed once and for all. This is because it is not a definitive final static condition, although after the step has been reached there is no turning back, because it would be anti-economic and corporate culture is now indelibly marked.

The sustainable management of a company is thus not the end of the story, an exact point to be registered, but rather a process of continuous change. What is a final target, however, is achieving those objectives that the company had set itself at the outset of the process, when it had planned its route to sustainability. In this sense it is fitting to mark the completion of Step 10 with a statement as a way of publicly announcing the results and sharing them with all the stakeholders. The end of the stage is also an opportunity to put forward new, more advanced objectives.

A note on corporate governance

The process illustrated in the ten steps requires a new approach to corporate governance. In some ways this will supplement and widen the perspective (broadened governance) of all the stakeholders' expectations and aspirations. Adopting sustainable practice implies a dialogue between the owners, management and other stakeholders. Obviously greater dialogue does not mean delegating decisions or responsibility in managing the business, which remains firmly in the hands of the owners and management.

Moreover, although not an inevitable outcome, on the path towards sustainability corporate governance may evolve from broadened governance, as described above, to participatory governance with a more active role for stakeholders in decision-making processes.

Cases of this kind can be found when there are three possible developments:
1) The change anticipated in Italy by the company law reform of 2003, which set up financial tools other than shares and bonds. They are, moreover, endowed with proprietary and administrative rights, for example, the right to vote on specific topics, such as appointing an independent member to the board of directors or

supervisory board or an auditor. This would be possible whenever the company offered the new tools to citizens or workers, giving them the right to vote on specific aspects of management.

2) Participation in the corporate capital by institutional investors specialised in socially responsible investment (SRI) or social, environmental and ethical investment (SEEI). One example would be an ethical fund or a socially responsible pension fund that has a large enough block of shares to be able to influence strategic decisions and administrative appointments. The logic can be applied to any company, independently of their quotation on the stock exchange, if the investor belongs to the category of sustainable private equity funds.

3) A company with committees made up of stakeholder representatives, when their role is not simply consultative but they also take part in decision-making. There are cases in practice and, albeit limited, also among Italian fashion companies, in which stakeholders are given some decision-making power, thus configuring the stakeholders' participation in corporate governance.

Conclusions

In conclusion, the very notion of sustainability is a continuously developing concept for which there are already several robust social responsibility methodologies. Pressure from regulators and markets on sustainability is destined to grow. There are all the reasons in the world why the Italian fashion system and its companies should decide as quickly as possible to tackle openly an issue that may be a solution to the now long-standing issue of how to guarantee the excellent quality of Italian products.

The challenge of sustainability means developing new modes of cooperation with stakeholders. But essentially it is simply a new chapter in the history of Italian competitiveness.

Select Bibliography

F. Guenza and D. Dal Maso, "La Corporate Social Responsibility nel Tessile Abbigliamento: Modelli virtuosi e buone pratiche per una competitività sostenibile; il ruolo della Grande Distribuzione Organizzata e del Dialogo Sociale", in *Quaderno di Fabrica Ethica*, 3/2007.

ICSR. Italian Centre for Social Responsibility, *Comitati Multi-Stakeholder e Responsabilità Sociale d'Impresa*, edited by M. Bartolomeo, 2009.

W. Edwards Deming, *Out of the Crisis,* Cambridge (MA) 1986.

FIVE.
ICONOGRAPHIC ATLAS

DIESEL - GLOBAL WARMING READY--------------

Founded by Renzo Rosso in 1978, this company has always stood out for its provocative advertising campaigns. With the slogans "Love Nature" and the "Global Warming Ready", in 2004 and 2007, respectively, Diesel proffered ironic, challenging reflections on problems of climate change.

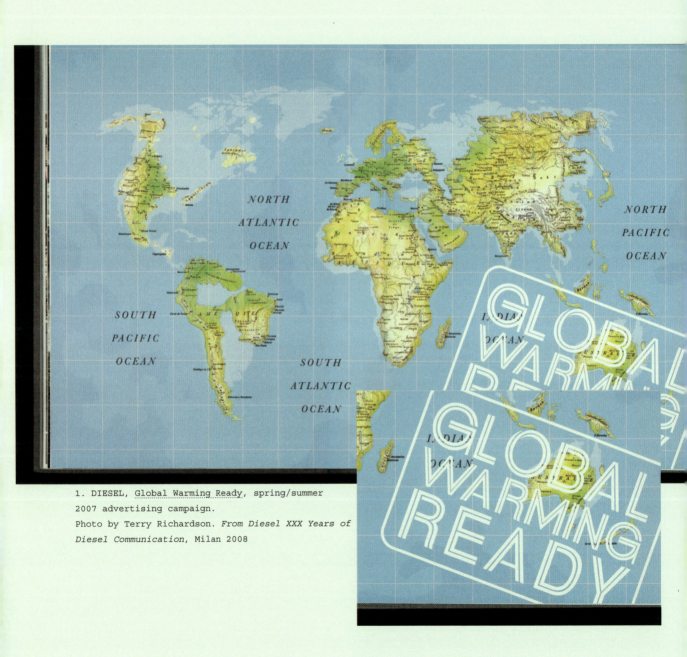

1. DIESEL, Global Warming Ready, spring/summer 2007 advertising campaign.
Photo by Terry Richardson. *From Diesel XXX Years of Diesel Communication*, Milan 2008

CLIMATE CHANGE------------------------------

In this case the title of a photographic service, "climate change", does not refer to global warming but to the changing seasons. The advert thus puns with the notion of climate change as an environmental challenge and the typical turnover in the fashion world from the winter to spring seasons.

2. Climate Change. Photo by Daniel Jackson.
Pages from *Vogue UK*, February 2010

3. DIESEL, <u>Global Warming Ready</u>, spring/summer 2007 advertising campaign.
Photo by Terry Richardson. From Diesel XXX Years of Diesel Communication, Milan 2008

CARMINA CAMPUS --------------------------------

Ilaria Venturini Fendi created Carmina Campus in late 2006.
Having worked for a long time in the family's celebrated fashion business, she left to run an organic farm. Her experience on the land combined with a background as a designer led to the creation of the Carmina Campus project.
The company has explored alternative paths in order to promote a new economics. Inspired by the most varied waste materials, it creates several lines of bags and clothing and furniture accessories. Each item is numbered and made by expert Italian artisans.
The interior of the RE(f)USE store in Rome is entirely made of reused materials.

www.carminacampus.org

4. CARMINA CAMPUS, Save Waste from Waste, a line of bags made starting from black plastic dustbin liners, doubled by a support endowing the material with a completely new consistency and dignity.
Courtesy Carmina Campus

ASAP--------------

The acronym for "As Sustainable As Possible", ASAP is a workshop dedicated to product research. While reducing waste, its mission is to create clothing and accessories with simple lines that do not follow seasonal trends. The various product lines are made of natural fibres and materials coloured using low environmental-impact vegetable dyes. Some garments are made with very high quality leftover material collected from warehouses of various Italian companies but no longer used because the quantities are too small for industrial production. All ASAP products are made in Italy with a short supply chain and to conserve the Italian artisan heritage. ASAP has two boutiques, in Rome and Paris, respectively.

www.asaplab.it

5. ASAP, d., dress made from leftover high-quality yarns and fabrics retrieved from selected companies. Courtesy ASAP
6. ASAP, Natural Dye Cashemere, cashmere accessories dyed with vegetable dyes and no chemical additives. Courtesy ASAP

NOON SOLAR---------------

Noon Solar is the result of a project set up by Jane Palmer and Marianne Fairbanks in Chicago in 2002. It came into being as a response to the impending war in Iraq. Feeling powerless in the face of the US military policy of going to war mainly for oil, the two designers came up with a solution to give people an alternative in the form of renewable solar power for small everyday requirements. Noon Solar bags are fitted with flexible solar panels, which provide enough energy to power a mobile phone or iPod.

www.noonstyle.com

7. NOON SOLAR, handbag with built-in solar panel. Photo by Jam.
From C. Smith and S. Topham, *XTream Fashion*, Munich 2005, p. 48

BANUQ------------------------------

The acronym for "Beautiful African Natural Unique Quality", BANUQ is a brand of menswear, founded in 2007 in Berlin by Italians Davide Grazioli and Mauro Pavesi.

The company set up a **sustainable supply chain** using **organic and biodynamic raw materials** processed in **ethically controlled environments.**

In 2011 Banuq launched a second, entirely Italian-made collection based on the use of raw materials from organic crops grown in Italy. The fabrics and dyeing processes are GOTS certified. BANUQ has been a member of MADE-BY since 2010.

www.banuq.com

8. BANUQ, Living on the Edge Collection, organic cotton shirts, coloured with eco-friendly dyes and necktie made from linen production leftovers and organic cotton, 2011. Courtesy BANUQ

9. BANUQ, Living on the Edge Collection, organic linen and biodynamic cotton jackets coloured with eco-friendly dyes, 2011. Courtesy BANUQ

10. BANUQ, Living on the Edge Collection, organic linen and biodynamic cotton suit. Photo by Kristian Geyr, 2011. Courtesy BANUQ

11. BANUQ, Living on the Edge Collection, biodynamic cotton poplin jacket. Photo by Kristian Geyr, 2011. Courtesy BANUQ

CANGIARI---------------------------------------

"Beauty is different"

Cangiari, meaning "to change" in Calabrian dialect, is a brand of womenswear created in 2009 by GOEL, a social consortium bringing together various firms from Locride and Piana di Gioia Tauro (Calabria); the consortium aim to **challenge the spread of Mafia organisations.** The Cangiari collections are **entirely made in Calabria** with the support of local social cooperatives and using **ICEA certified organic fabrics.**

The company's first boutique, Spazio Cangiari, was opened in Milan in 2010 in a building confiscated from the *'ndrangheta* (Calabrian mafia).

In 2011 the artistic director of the brand, Marina Spadafora, launched the spring/summer collection in Milan.

www.cangiari.it

12. CANGIARI, detail of a handloom used to weave Cangiari fabrics. Courtesy Cangiari
13. CANGIARI, spring/summer 2011 collection, muga silk top, jacket tailored from cloth made on a handloom, organic cotton trousers and slacks.
Photo by Toni Meneguzzo. Courtesy Cangiari

14. CANGIARI, spring/summer 2011 collection, organic linen dress with inserts, made on handloom. Photo by Toni Meneguzzo. Courtesy Cangiari

15. CANGIARI, spring/summer 2011 collection, organic cotton outfit. Photo by Toni Meneguzzo. Courtesy Cangiari

DOSA--

Dosa was founded by Christina Kim, a designer of Korean origin who lives and works in Los Angeles.
Having begun working in 1982, Christina Kim stands out for her respect for the environment and the people involved in the manufacturing process. In her projects, she uses recycled and organic fabrics, at times in collaboration with non-governmental organisations. In Italy the designer held an exhibition entitled *Organic, Recycled, Handmade: Fashion and Ethics in the Work of Christina Kim*, at the Museo Internazionale e Biblioteca della Musica, Bologna in 2008.

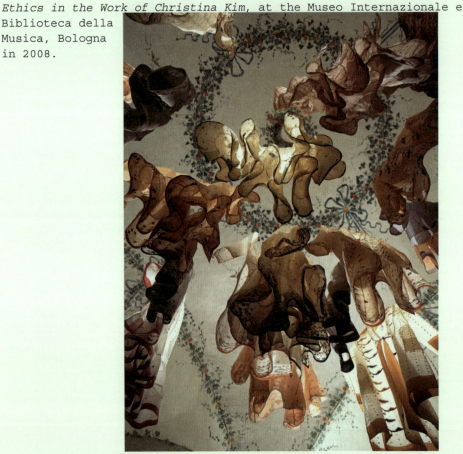

16. DOSA, handmade pure cotton clothes woven with a typical Bangladesh method involving the use of a supplementary weft to form a geometric pattern. *Organic, Recycled, Handmade: Fashion and Ethics in the Work of Christina Kim*, Museo Internazionale e Biblioteca della Musica, Bologna 2008. Photo by Mark Schoole. Courtesy Dosa

17. DOSA, installation consisting of around 85 "milagros". Each milagro is a long thread from which hang small shapes - hearts, moons and stars - handmade by an association of Indian woman using recycled fabrics and paillettes. *Organic, Recycled, Handmade: Fashion and Ethics in the Work of Christina Kim*, Museo Internazionale e Biblioteca della Musica, Bologna 2008. Photo by Raymond Meier. Courtesy Dosa

18. DOSA, collage of samples documenting Dosa projects since 1993. Each sample, made from various kinds of materials, is hand-sown to a silk support. *Organic, Recycled, Handmade: Fashion and Ethics in the Work of Christina Kim*, Museo Internazionale e Biblioteca della Musica, Bologna 2008. Photo by Raymond Meier. Courtesy Dosa

MARIA VITTORIA SARGENTINI: JERSEY² ------------------

Jersey² is a project conceived by Italian designer Maria Vittoria Sargentini. The geometrical figure of the square is elaborated in various sizes to give rise to flat shapes which, when draped over the body, create different lengths and volumes.

Jersey² is entirely made of Milkofil and Lenpur, two fibres with different eco features extracted from milk proteins and wood pulp, respectively.

www.marvielab.com

19-22. MARVIELAB, Jersey² Project, clothes made with Milkofil and Lenpur.
Photo by Ilaria D'atri (Lost & Found Studio). Courtesy Marvielab

SENSITIVE® ECO PRINT --------------------------

This ecological printing method developed by the Italian textile company Eurojersey has several advantages, especially in environmental terms.

Thanks to a paste with a special solution enabling the colour to anchor to the textile, ECO PRINT interacts with the plain ground to reproduced tone on tone effects or contrasts.

This printing method has no need for vaporising or textile washing stages, thus bringing savings on energy and large quantities of water (around 50 litres for every metre of fabric). Moreover, thanks to the reduction in dyes and chemicals, the environmental impact on wastewater is less than in conventional printing processes.

www.sensitivecosystem.it

23. EUROJERSEY, logo. Courtesy Eurojersey
24. EUROJERSEY, SENSITIVE® ECO PRINT printed fabric.
Courtesy Eurojersey

FROM SOMEWHERE -

This London-based womenswear brand was set up by Orsola di Castro and Filippo Ricci in 1997. From Somewhere garments are one-off and created with high quality raw materials that are strictly second-hand or textile industry surpluses.
The garments are produced in limited editions in England and Italy, where From Somewhere relies on the collaboration of the Rinascere social cooperative, whose mission is to give work to disadvantaged people. Besides working as a designer, since September 2006, Orsola di Castro and her companion Filippo Ricci, with the support of the British Fashion Council, have curated Estethica, the section in the London Fashion Week entirely dedicated to sustainable fashion.

www.fromsomewhere.co.uk

25. FROM SOMEWHERE, spring/summer 2004 collection. Photo by Filippo Ricci.
Courtesy Form Somewhere
26. FROM SOMEWHERE, spring/summer 2003 collection. Photo by Luke White.
Courtesy Form Somewhere
27. FROM SOMEWHERE, spring/summer 2004 collection. Photo by Filippo Ricci.
Courtesy From Somewhere

FROM SOMEWHERE

197

FREITAG----------------------------

The Swiss company uses materials normally found on the road: old tarpaulins, car safety belts, bicycle tubes and airbags. The company was created in Zurich when the two Freitag brothers wanted to design a functional, waterproof and resistant bag that was also the result of a design process based on recycling.
Since the Freitag products are made using canvas materials with different colours, writings and sizes, each accessory is one-off.

www.freitag.ch

28-30. FREITAG, stages in making a bag. Photo by Noë Flum. Courtesy Freitag
31. FREITAG, diagram illustrating the company concept. Photo by Noë Flum. Courtesy Freitag

BY GENTUCCA BINI--

Milanese designer Gentucca Bini's
latest project literally involves a
process of **re-labelling**: outmoded
collections and garments are revisited
in the Gentucca Bini style, at times
with slight but significant changes, at
other times with radical alterations.
The old label is flanked
by the Gentucca Bini
brand to **bring back
to life ready-to-wear
clothes** and collections
that otherwise would have
been thrown out, with
obvious reductions in
waste.

www.by-project.com

32-34. BY GENTUCCA BINI, event
at *Pitti Uomo* 77, January 2010.
Photo by Giovanni
Giannoni. Courtesy Pitti
Immagine
35. BY GENTUCCA BINI,
installation at *Touch! Neozone e
Cloudine*, September 2010. Photo
by Rocco Patella. Courtesy Pitti
Immagine

LUISA CEVESE RIEDIZIONI-------------------------------

Luisa Cevese's Riedizioni brand is found on bags and household
items. The accessories are made from scraps of textiles
and production leftovers combined with plastic material
of various kinds. After having worked for a long time in
a major Italian textile company, and aware of the enormous
quantity of leftovers produced, Luisa Cevese decided to use
scraps as raw material with a view to recycling and
saving on waste. Large pieces of unused and damaged fabric, yarns,
selvages,
small pieces
of irregular
textiles and
production
scraps are
juxtaposed
and merged in
combinations
decided each
time by a
machine.

www.riedizioni.
com

36. LUISA CEVESE RIEDIZIONI SPECIALI, little prayer, wool, cotton and polyurethane,
2001. Courtesy Luisa Cevese Riedizioni
37. LUISA CEVESE RIEDIZIONI, handbag made of polyurethane and linen selvage. Courtesy
Luisa Cevese Riedizioni

38. LUISA CEVESE RIEDIZIONI, handbag made of polyurethane and pieces of fur. Courtesy Luisa Cevese Riedizioni

39. LUISA CEVESE RIEDIZIONI, handbag made of polyurethane and silk sari. Courtesy Luisa Cevese Riedizioni

40. LUISA CEVESE RIEDIZIONI, handbag made of polyurethane and silk selvage. Courtesy Luisa Cevese Riedizioni

MOMABOMA--

Founded by Maurizio Longati, this Bolognese company creates
handbags and accessories starting from the pages of old magazines
and newspapers.
Each publication is divided by category and state of conservation,
and the pages are catalogued according to the graphics and
colours. After being carefully selected, the pages are stuck
together, attached to a polypropylene mesh and treated with resin
to obtain a resistant waterproof material.
The collection's nostalgic feel is imparted by the classic design
that effectively combines tradition and recycled material.

www.momaboma.it

41-42. MOMABOMA, stages in making Momaboma handbags. Photo by Nicola Licata. Courtesy
Momaboma
43-45. MOMABOMA, spring/summer 2011 collection. Photo by Alessandra Leonardi.
Courtesy Momaboma

46-49. MOMABOMA, stages in making Momaboma handbags. Photo
by Nicola Licata. Courtesy Momaboma

PIETRA PISTOLETTO ----------------------

Pietra Pistoletto launched her Pietra brand in 1994. The Turin designer makes the concept of recycling the key feature of her work.

Recurrent elements in Pietra Pistoletto's designs are socks, stockings and underwear that are converted into long dresses but also skirts and tops; these ready-to-wear clothes combine the principles of recycling with an aesthetic appeal.

Here recycling not only means using second-hand materials but also redesigning industrial scraps to become the source of new accessories, dubbed by the designer herself as "anti-jewels". In this case the value comes from the underlying ethical principles rather than the preciousness of the materials. The garments and jewels are usually one-offs, handmade by Pietra herself.

www.pietrapistoletto.com

50. PIETRA PISTOLETTO, Slip Wedding Dress, 1996. Wedding dress handmade from samples of women's underwear, the Fondazione Mudima fashion show, Milan. Courtesy Pietra Pistoletto
51. PIETRA PISTOLETTO, street market-style display, Museo Pecci, Prato 1996. Courtesy Pietra Pistoletto

52. PIETRA PISTOLETTO, <u>Dress - Rug - Light</u>, 2004. Dress entirely hand-sown with scraps and samples of socks. Photo by Max Tomasinelli. Courtesy Pietra Pistoletto

MINÄ PERHONEN----------------------------

Minä Perhonen was created in 1995 as a result of Japanese designer
Akira Minagawa's passionate interest in Scandinavian culture. In
Finish the brand name means "I" (*minä*) and "butterfly" (*perhonen*).
Akira Minagawa lives and works in Tokyo,
where she produces garments with the support
of small workshops and tailors who still
work using artisan methods and ancient
sewing techniques, thus keeping alive a
tradition of hands-on knowledge.
Akira Minagawa's approach is to create very
high quality clothes outside the frenetic pace
of fast-changing fashions.

www.mina-perhonem.jp

53. MINÄ PERHONEN, 2008.
From S. Black, *Eco Chic: The
Fashion Paradox*, London 2008
54-55. MINÄ PERHONEN, launch
of the autumn/winter 2007-
2008 collection.
From L. Eceiza Nebreda,
Atlante della moda, Modena
2009

465
minä perhonen

467
minä perhonen

ROYAH--

The Royah project was set up in Kabul in 2005 thanks to the support of Gabriella Ghidoni and Arte-fatto Onlus, a non-profit association dedicated to conserving local artisan skills in developing countries.

Inspired by a thousand-year-old Afghan tradition, Royah makes a refined line of women's outerwear and other clothing by reworking ancient Persian and Islamic patterns. The garments are made by a Kabul women's cooperative, whereas the style is designed by Gabriella Ghidoni.

www.royah.org

56, 59, 61. ROYAH, autumn/winter 2010-2011 collection.
Courtesy Royah Design Archive
57, 58, 60. ROYAH, woman at work in the Kabul workshop.
Courtesy Royah Design Archive

CLEAN CLOTHES CAMPAIGN - CAMPAGNA ABITI PULITI-----

This association of organisations from the trade union world and
NGOs has branches in fourteen European countries.
Created in 1989, Clean Clothes Campaign can rely on a network of
over 200 farmers in various manufacturing countries in order to
establish and plan objectives and strategies in line with the
association's mission: i.e. improve working conditions
of people in the production process of the textile and clothing
sector.
Campagna Abiti Puliti is the Italian section of the Clean Clothes
Campaign.

www.abitipuliti.org

62. CAMPAGN ABITI PULITI, logo.
Courtesy Campagna Abiti Puliti

MARKS AND SPENCER --------------------------

The care label on Marks & Spencer garments invites owners to wash the clothes at low temperature so as to save on energy.

The label is part of Plan A, an ambitious campaign launched by Stuart Rose in 2007 with the aim of making Marks & Spencer the most sustainable retailer worldwide by the end of 2015.

63. MARKS AND SPENCER, care label. From S. Black, *Eco Chic: The Fashion Paradox*, London 2008

AMERICAN APPAREL----------------------

The Los Angeles-based casual wear company was founded in 2000 by Dov Charney.
American Apparel's manufacturing policy stands out because of its total vertical integration of people working in one place – downtown Los Angeles. In clear contrast to the phenomenon of relocating, the American Apparel business model guarantees traceability and transparency as well as respect for working and environmental standards. The garments are entirely designed and made in the Californian factory and indeed American Apparel claims that the fact their clothes are "Made in downtown LA" is its great strength.

Advertising images from
American Apparel

RIGHT:
American Apparel advert
highlighting the vertical
business structure and
"Made in LA" philosophy
of the company

— 188 —

www.americanapparel.net

64. AMERICAN APPAREL, diagram illustrating the company manufacturing philosophy of vertical integration. From S. Black, *Eco Chic: The Fashion Paradox*, London 2008

www.americanapparel.net

American Apparel®

production and pro-labour policies, American Apparel has become a cool brand amongst its target market, also known for its upfront and sexually charged advertising using company employees—often photographed by Charney, which commentators have seen as contradictory to the rest of its philosophy. A team of six workers, paid on piecework, can make a t-shirt in 11 seconds. With over 1.3 million garments made annually American Apparel is now the biggest clothing manufacturer in the US.

American Apparel adverts, such as the one above, often feature unstyled candid shots of employees.

ECOLABEL-------------------------------
Introduced in 1992, Ecolabel is the European Union's label
of environmental certification. In assessing the
environmental impact, Ecolabel criteria take into account the
entire product life cycle, including aspects such as energy
consumption, water and atmospheric pollution, and waste
production. In 1999 textile products were also included in the
categories of certifiable goods.
.

ec.europa.eu/environment/ecolabel

65. ECOLABEL, logo.
Courtesy Ecolabel

This major Italian yarn manufacturer has invested in the development of thread from high-tech sustainable fibres, especially by using biopolymers such as Milkofil, derived from milk protein and Lenpur, made from cellulose. The company permanently allocates resources to experimentation in the application of new eco-friendly materials in spinning by collaborating with fibre producers, universities and research centres.

www.filatimaclodio.it

66. Filati Maclodio, presentation of yarns. Courtesy Filati Maclodio

THE ETHICAL FASHION SHOW----------------------

The Ethical Fashion Show is a major international trade fair entirely dedicated to the sustainable fashion sector. Held annually in Paris since 2004, it provides an opportunity to get together for designers and producers from various parts of the world, all with the same deep commitment. The Ethical Fashion Show has developed its own system of icons to identify and describe visually the ethical criteria of each exhibitor present at the fair.

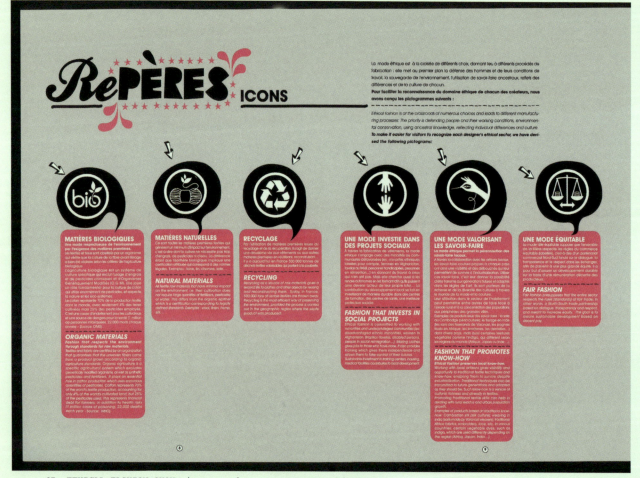

67. ETHICAL FASHION SHOW, icons used to represent graphically the ethical criteria of the exhibitors at the show. From the catalogue of *The Ethical Fashion Show* 2008, graphic design by Monique Design

RADICIGROUP------------------------

This Italian company has manufacturing and commercial facilities in Europe, Asia and North and South America. Its businesses include chemicals, plastic materials, synthetic fibres and textiles. Its products are used in the clothing, sport, furnishing, automobile, electronics and household appliances sectors.

RadiciGroup has developed many practical programmes inspired by the values of sustainability and social responsibility. They include the 2009 RadiciGroup for Sustainability initiative, whose aim was "to raise awareness in people about sustainability in life styles and working methods, and as a key element in the group's growth".

www.radicigroup.com

68. RADICIGROUP, Operation Twenty[4]. Courtesy RadiciGroup.

C.L.A.S.S.---------------------------------------

Acronym of "Creativity Lifestyle And Sustainable Synergy",
C.L.A.S.S. is an international eco platform founded in 2007 with
the aim of promoting the use of eco-sustainable materials
in fashion and design. The three company showrooms in
Milan, London and New York, respectively, are meeting places for
designers, companies and buyers in search of a vast selection of
textiles, yarns and finished products.

www.c-l-a-s-s.org

69. C.L.A.S.S., logo.
Courtesy C.L.A.S.S.

CITTADELLARTE FASHION B.E.S.T.--------------------

B.E.S.T. is the acronym of "Bio Ethical Sustainable Trend", an
initiative created in 2009 by the Fondazione Pistoletto for the
purpose of promoting actions to develop fashion according to the
principles of sustainability.

www.cittadellarte.it

70. B.E.S.T., logo.
Courtesy B.E.S.T.

C--------------------

71. <u>Super Nature</u>, cover of *i-D*, winter 2009. Photo by Alasdair McLellan

72. <u>The natural touch</u>, express fashion, concept 2Som Studio. Photo by Bloonie Fotografie. Pages from *View 2 Magazine*, 02, summer 2007

-Nature-
Love it while it lasts

Join the Diesel Society of Nature Lovers at
www.diesel.com

73. DIESEL, Love Nature, spring/summer 2004 advertising campaign. Photo by Henrik Halvarsson. From *Diesel XXX Years of Diesel Communication*, Milan 2008

Eco System

Ecology and industrial know-how fuse. Mock wood PV

74. Farmlife, casual wear forecast, directions and concept by Tony Bannister (Scout). Pages from *Textile View Magazine*, 85, spring 2009

75. Eco System. Photo by Alexis Lecomte, concept and design by Anne Liberati and Soon Luu. Pages from *View 2 Magazine*, 03, winter 2007

76. Express yourself /Eco-friendly couriers. Photo by Alexis Lecomte, concept and design by Anne Liberati and Soon Luu. Pages from *View 2 Magazine*, 08, summer 2010

77. "Curiosity ecologico". Pages from "Shopping in Vogue", supplement to *Vogue Italia*, 690, February 2008

EXPRESS YOURSELF /
ECO-FRIENDLY COURIERS

HIGHLIGHTS
- Yellow rackets
- Decafeinnated blacks
- Grilled PVC
- Spicy reins
- Enamelled Kevlar
- Undergood zips

1. DORLET (F) 2. LAMPO (I) 3. MANIFATTURA DI DREME (I) 4. DEPA (P) 5. PRERISTOS SHARELY (F) 6. TEXTCART (G) 7. BESTAL (F)

229

Greenacres

Greenacres

The greens we have focused on in the trend section are actually softened and more greyed-off than these, but we feel there is room to flash in these crisper and more vibrant shades. The eco messages continue.

Going green

Going green

Consumerism with a sense of conscience is a crucial topic and helping the planet is an important facet of new morality. This movement is reflected symbolically by embracing green. It can be used in colour blocks for a whole outfit or just in touches, bringing a shot of vitality and a positive vibe.

78. <u>Greenacres</u>, colour and fabric forecast, concept by D. Cipher. Pages from *Textile View Magazine*, 89, spring 2010

79. <u>Going green</u>, street fashion. Photo and concept by Tal Lancman. Pages from *Textile View Magazine*, 76, winter 2006

80. <u>Living green</u>. Photo by Steven Meisel, fashion editor Karl Templer. Pages from *Vogue Italia*, 690, February 2008

81. <u>Absolute Green</u>. Photo by Alexis Lecomte, concept and design by Anne Liberati and Soon Luu. Pages from *View 2 Magazine*, 07, winter 2009

82. <u>Green goddess</u>, Gift aid, edited by Sarah Harris and Calgary Avansino. Pages from *Vogue UK*, December 2009

83. MARITHÉ ET FRANÇOIS GIRBAUD, spring/summer 2007 advertising campaign.
Photo by Jackie Nickerson. Pages from *Vogue Italia*, 679, March 2007

MARITHÉ+FRANÇOIS GIRBAUD È FIERA DI SOSTENERE SEEDS OF PEACE
FUCINA DEI FUTURI LEADER DI PACE

.... Prepress
Fotolito Veneta, San Martino Buonalbergo (Verona)

.... Printed by
Studio Fasoli, Verona
for Marsilio Editori® Spa in Venezia

edition
10 9 8 7 6 5 4 3 2 1

year
2012 2013 2014 2015 2016

Along its entire industrial production chain, from chemicals to plastics and synthetic fibres, RadiciGroup's commitment to sustainable action entails demonstrating respect for its stakeholders, reporting corporate responsibility according to *Global Reporting Initiative (GRI)* guidelines, reducing greenhouse gas emissions and energy consumption, increasing the use of renewable source energy and increasing the use of materials from the recycling of both post-consumer waste and its own production waste/rejects. In 2011 the share of renewable source electric power used by RadiciGroup rose to 40%. In the same year, the share of recycled materials originating from its own polyamide production chain was 15%. RadiciGroup has developed products using renewable source materials, products made from post-consumer recycled materials and other products helping to lower CO_2 emissions. The Group is implementing methods, such as *Life Cycle Assessment (LCA)*, to measure and quantify product performance in terms of environmental impact. It is committed to publishing *Environmental Product Declarations (EPDs)* for its products, according to the specific requirements set forth in the *Product Category Rules (PCR)*. Also important is the Group's active participation in sustainability issues as a member of industry associations and organizations. In the communities where its production sites are located, RadiciGroup supports projects and events on environmental protection and sustainability themes and strives to raise the environmental awareness of its employees by promoting a culture of sustainability – all the while, respectful of local communities, people and cultures.

This is how RadiciGroup is addressing the sustainability challenge. With concrete actions. Actions that the Group illustrates in a simple and clear manner in the video *RadiciGroup for Sustainability – The Cartoon*. With this corporate communication video RadiciGroup intends to provide all its stakeholders, not only engineers and sustainable development experts, a cross-section of its activities on the sustainability front.

www.radicigroup.com